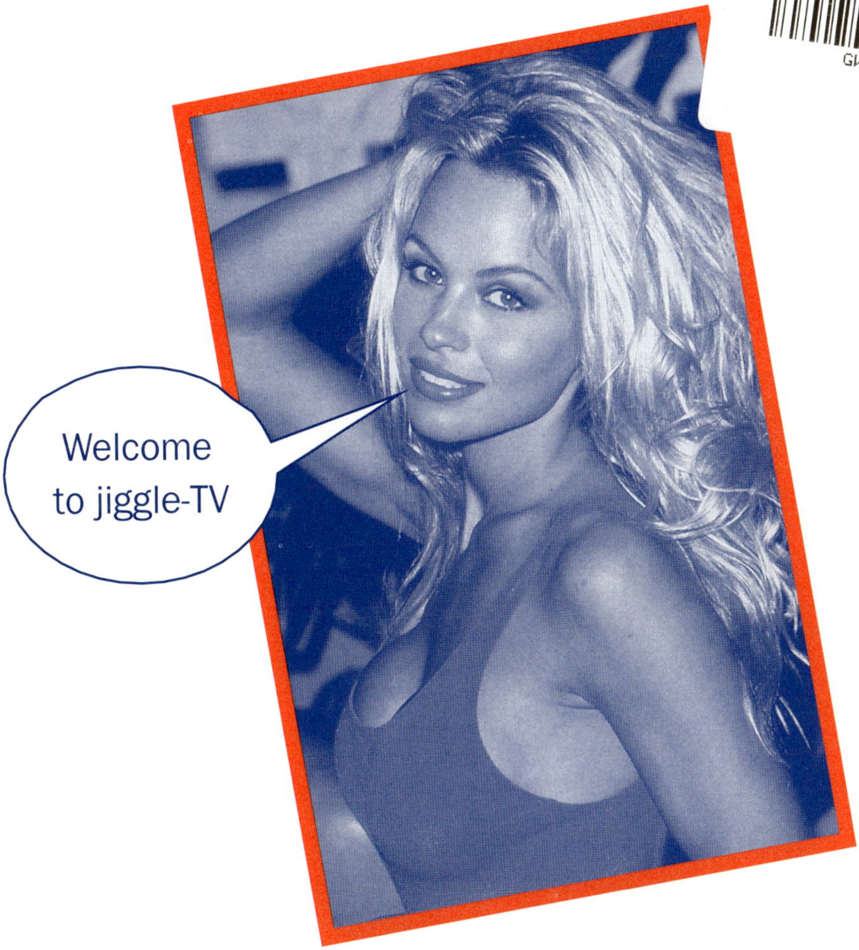
Welcome
to jiggle-TV

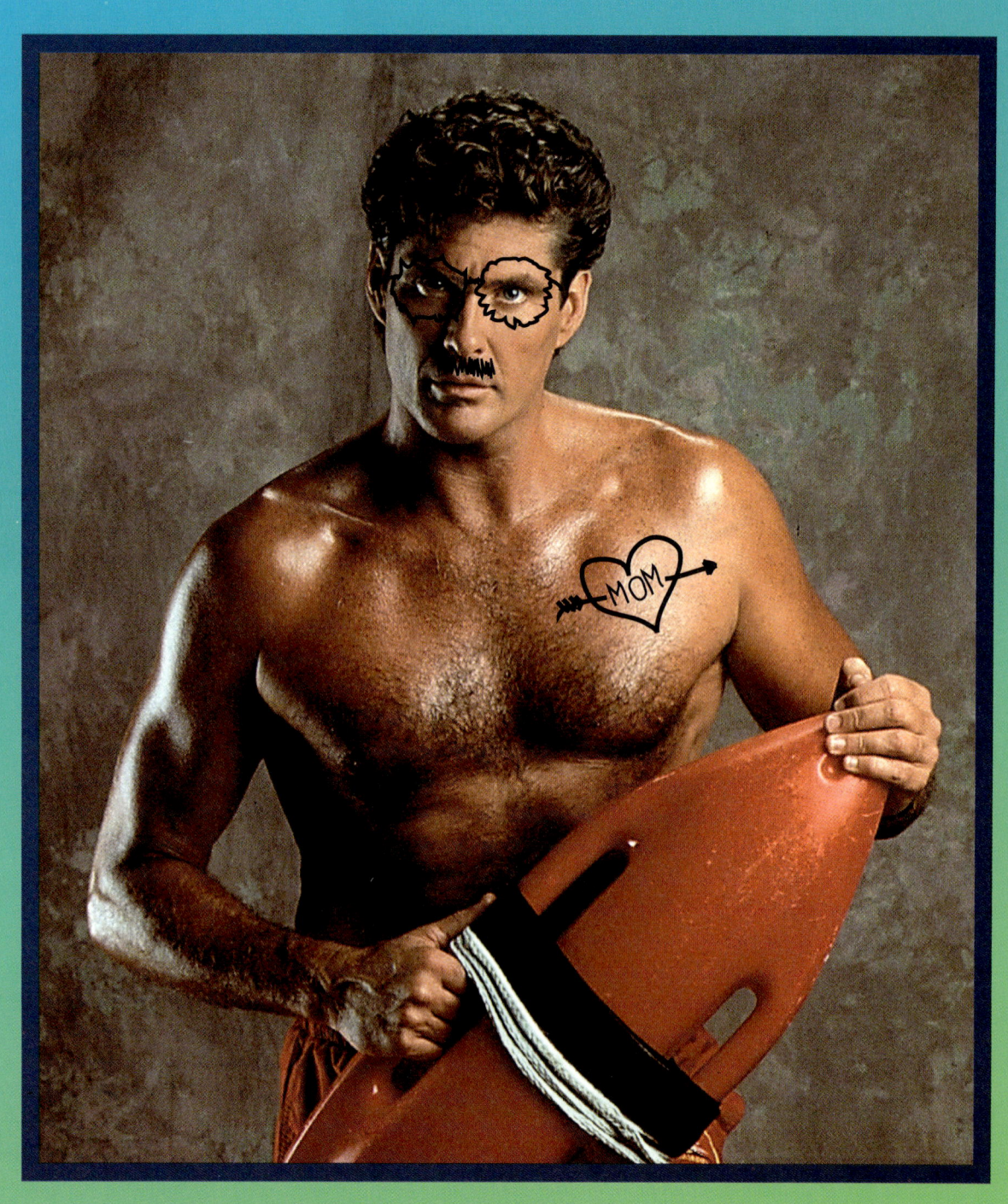

'Anyone who makes fun of *Baywatch*
is doing it out of ignorance.'
David Hasselhoff

# PLANET BAYWATCH

*the unofficial guide
to the new world order*

**Brendan Baber
and Eric Spitznagel**

Michael O'Mara Books Limited

First published in Great Britain in 1996 by
Michael O'Mara Books Limited
9 Lion Yard
Tremadoc Road
London SW4 7NQ

Copyright © 1996 Brendan Baber & Eric Spitznagel

All rights reserved. No part of this publication may be reproduced, stored in a retrieval system, or transmitted by any means, without the prior permission in writing of the publisher, nor be otherwise circulated in any form of binding or cover other than that in which it is published and without a similar condition including this condition being imposed on the subsequent purchaser.

The right of Brendan Baber and Eric Spitznagel to be identified as the authors of this work has been jointly asserted by them in accordance with the Copyright, Designs and Patents Act 1988.

A CIP catalogue record for this book is available from the British Library

ISBN 1-85479-654-2

1 3 5 7 9 10 8 6 4 2

Typeset and Designed by Robert Updegraff
Origination by Adelphi Graphics
Printed in Great Britain by Jarrold Book Printing, Thetford

# WHAT IS PLANET BAYWATCH?

*Baywatch* saves lives. Tabloids abound with stories about children who saved pets using techniques learned from watching *Baywatch*. And, the Baywatch Production Company keeps a record of newspaper accounts of people who saved lives because of their show, as well as letters from grateful parents and children.

Remember, *this* is the show that is supposed to be nothing more than breasts, buttocks and slow-motion jiggling. And please bear in mind that *this* is the show most people won't admit they watch. (Of course, we know they're lying. The numbers and ratings reveal that a massive chunk of the world is watching *Baywatch*, and then lying through their teeth when asked about it.) And yet this show, this behemoth of American culture, this improbably profitable beast of Los Angeles capitalism at its worst, *this* is the show that's saving lives?

Let's get down to basics: what is this thing that hulks toward us from the beaches of California? Why does it deliver trashy, tasteless thong bikinis from its right hand, and life-affirming aphorisms from its left? What does it want? When will it be satisfied? And most importantly, just how goddamn big is it?

That much, at least, we can answer.

*Baywatch* is broadcast to over 2.4 billion people per week, of whom anywhere from 60 per cent to 80 per cent may be watching. So we're talking about a viewership of roughly two billion souls, give or take a few hundred million. *Baywatch* is broadcast in 120 countries, and on every continent except Antarctica (where you could probably catch it on a VCR in the rec room at McMurdo Base anyway). In the Amazon river basin the locals crank up gas generators to watch it on black and white television sets. In Russia, Australia, Zimbabwe, Morocco, Pakistan and Outer Mongolia they're all holding their breath to see if Mitch and Stephanie will ever get it on. And maybe picking up valuable tips on CPR (Cardiovascular Pulmonary Resuscitation, to you). The mind boggles.

But we're inundated with big numbers every day, so figures like 'two billion' slide right off our collective consciousness, leaving nothing but a greasy patch of numbness to mark their passing. Let's make a few comparisons to put it all in perspective:

According to the *1995 Britannica Book of the Year*, there are roughly one billion Muslims in the world, which makes Allah half as pervasive as *Baywatch*.

*Forget about your religious wars and ethnic cleansing. Come on over to the California beach and have some sun and fun.*

*Around the world viewers are holding their breath to see if Mitch and Stephanie will ever get it on.*

The global population of Christians is estimated at 1.8 billion, so it's a toss-up as to whether Jesus Christ or Lieutenant Mitch Buchannon will win the popularity contest — but Mitch's ratings are increasing more quickly. Baywatchers outnumber Jews by at least 100 to 1, since there are only 18 million adherents to the Torah. Democracy is much less widespread than *Baywatch*, since only one billion people are living in 'free' countries. (In case you were wondering, that means that *Baywatch* is twice as successful as voting.) If you haven't gotten the picture yet, we'll say it straight out: *Baywatch* is not a part of world culture; it *is* the world's culture. It is not merely the most successful TV show in the world; it is the most popular single cultural phenomenon *ever*.

*Baywatch*'s critics are deluded fools. It does not matter if they think it's crap. Frankly, it doesn't matter if *you* think it's crap. Two billion viewers can't be wrong, even if they are huddled around gas generators in the rain forest.

But the question lingers: just what is so special about *Baywatch*? We can all appreciate the absurd aesthetics of Pamela Anderson Lee's impressive breast implants and David Hasselhoff's well-oiled sprints to the rescue, but is that enough to attract the huge following that *Baywatch* has inspired? The French magazine *Max* recently referred to the show as 'une allagorie vivante,' or 'a living allegory.' It's a description that may be closer to the truth than any of us know.

The world of *Baywatch* is a utopia. The sun always shines and the beach is always bustling with happy, exceedingly attractive people. There are no problems that cannot be overcome by the governing body, or 'lifeguards.' There are no racial tensions, sexual diseases or drug abuse on the *Baywatch* team. Everyone has enough to eat, a roof over their heads and a satisfying means of employment. Differences of opinion are easily settled, and there are no secrets among fellow Baywatchers. Life is a team effort, a team that works and makes everybody's lives better. And most important of all, almost no one *ever* dies on *Baywatch*. The lifeguards save everybody. No matter what kind of trouble you get into, they will be 'there for you,' to ensure your survival and continuing presence in the sun-filled paradise of eternal youth.

It's a comforting vision, and a vision that most of the world can easily relate to. Whether you're a right-wing gun fanatic, a French pseudo-intellectual, or a peasant living in a shack made out of dung, you can appreciate and even desire the giddy idealism that *Baywatch* preaches. That's why *Baywatch*'s power over our collective fantasies is so terrifying. If *Baywatch* is the only world-view that we can all agree on, how long will it take before David Hasselhoff and company make the next logical leap and assume complete political and moral control over every nation? Who could possibly refuse the prospect of a world government, one that will unite us all under the promise of eternal Californian sun and fun. Under a *Baywatch* regime, there will be no more wars, no more disease, no more *death*. The dream of Planet Baywatch is very real, and it is coming faster than you think.

*Two billion viewers can't be wrong.*

# The Beach, the Babes and the American Dream:
# Ten Truths Learned From Watching BAYWATCH

So there you are in Outer Mongolia, hanging out in the yurt, huddled around the tribe's only television, and like the rest of the world you're watching The Show. Odds are you'll never actually meet an American, so what conclusions are you drawing about this mythical race with eternal tans and perfect teeth? We examined a few episodes at random and attempted to decipher exactly what these Noble Savages have learned about us from watching *Baywatch*.

## I
Americans spend 15% of their day running in slow motion on the beach.

## II
Americans drown twice in the average hour.

## III
However, despite this habit of inhaling water, CPR always works, and they never really die, except maybe when they have cancer.

## IV
People in the U.S. look thoughtfully at the ocean for an average of fifteen seconds after being told anything important.

## V
The majority of American women have abnormally large breasts and they are worshipped via close-ups for an average of two minutes and thirteen seconds per hour.

## VI
Americans never worry about getting enough to eat, but fat people are unreliable and sometimes evil.

## VII
When swimming in California, you are more likely to be attacked by jewel thieves or taken hostage by terrorists than drown.

## VIII
Most activity that takes place outside the beach occurs in montages, and lasts no longer than two minutes.

## IX
Although all Americans, especially lifeguards, complain that they are poor, they all have expensive sports cars and large, luxurious homes.

## X
Motorboats, unlike cars, will not talk back to David Hasselhoff.

# 28½ Reasons Why BAYWATCH is the Greatest TV Show in the History of Humanity!

What is the secret to *Baywatch*? What does it have that less successful works like *Friends* and *Hamlet* don't? Why does it vault over trade barriers and tribal wars, going places no show has gone before?

How does it transcend racial, religious and ethnic differences, to be embraced by Bantu, Briton and Bengali alike?

There can be no single reason. But there just might be 28 ½.

**1.** David Hasselhoff.

**2.** It's managed to distract the Germans so they haven't been able to start another world war.

**3.** They won't show us Pamela Anderson Lee's tattoo, but they're more than happy to show us her buttocks and breasts.

**4.** It has never been used as an example of Hollywood indecency by the Moral Majority or the political right although it shows more flesh than any other show in syndication.

**5.** The show's success has convinced Hasselhoff that he can also be a rock star.

**6.** The only major aesthetic change that *Baywatch* has made since its first season is a decrease in the number of shark attacks.

**7.** If you watch enough episodes, it has the same effect on your system as crystal meth.

**8.** Meaning to say, it makes you paranoid, violent and horny.

**9.** In some parts of Europe and Massachusetts, Jeremy Jackson is considered sexy.

**10.** Yasmine Bleeth claimed that the reason she's never posed naked for *Playboy* is 'I've never been able to go along with the idea of taking your clothes off for public consumption.'

**11.** Even though David Hasselhoff is getting older and fatter, he still refuses to put his shirt on.

**12.** They've paid 'homage' to *Casablanca*, *From Here to Eternity* and *Gilligan's Island*.

**13.** The chorus of 'I'll Be There,' the opening song to every episode, is one of the greatest examples of white-trash stadium rock ever recorded.

**14.** A Muslim journalist described the show as 'healthy and clean.'

**15.** When Pamela Anderson Lee runs in slow motion, gravity's cruel and powerful control is fully understood.

**16.** The show was actually canceled after its first season.

**17.** A tuberculosis clinic in Soweto, South Africa, has named a ward after David Hasselhoff.

**18.** David Hasselhoff gets more on-screen romances than his younger, more attractive co-stars.

**19.** It is seen in Outer Mongolia but not, curiously, Inner Mongolia.

**20.** The grand prize of an official *Baywatch* contest was a script from the show.

**21.** Hasselhoff has five gold records in Germany.

**22.** Hasselhoff once described the show as *Knight Rider* on the beach.

**23.** They've had two episodes about midgets and an episode about a giant.

**24.** Some of its detractors have taken to calling it Babewatch, Buttwatch, Beaverwatch and GynoVision.

**25.** They don't know they're funny.

*CPR saved his life.*

**26.** When they try to be funny, it's even funnier because they're not.

**27.** Pamela Anderson Lee actually expects us to believe that she's only had 'a little' plastic surgery.

**28.** A young Australian fan who learned about CPR from the show used it to save the life of his drowning pet bunny.

**28 1/2.** Pamela Anderson Lee agreed to be the prototype for Pammy Cola, a soft drink that comes in an hourglass bottle that's supposed to resemble Pam's curvy body.

# Mitch Buchannon

Who is Mitch Buchannon? We know him best as a highly skilled lifeguard, a devoted father and a lover of beach babes. But there's something else about him, something that we can't quite put our finger on. There's an undeniable other-worldly quality to him that can't be fully explained. Sure, he faces the same moral and physical challenges that affect all characters on *Baywatch*, but there is something about him that suggests an almost divine presence. Maybe it's the calm center he manages to maintain even in the most desperate situations. Maybe it's the ethereal wisdom he displays when all hope seems to be lost. Or maybe it's just those flirty eyes. Whatever the reason, we can't help but think that there's a lot more to Mitch than he's letting on.

The closest we've come to getting a glimpse into the *real* Mitch Buchannon was a scene in the episode titled 'Submersion.' In it, Mitch runs on the beach and feels remorseful about a child he was unable to save from drowning. He drops to his knees in the surf and screams at the heavens. The muscles on his chest ripple and throb as he unleashes his terrible fury. Hardly a picture of frailty, he seems to be mourning more for the lost child than his supposed botched rescue. He's like a sad God, agonizing over the Fall of Man. Although He is all-powerful, He cannot protect his children from their own mortality. He weeps for us, but it is all part of a Holy Plan that only He understands.

Mitch giveth, and Mitch taketh away.

*He's like a sad God, agonizing over the Fall of Man.*

# Raw Data

*Mr Ripple-Pecks*

**Sex:** Male
**Age:** 30-ish
**Career Prior to Joining Baywatch:** Navy SEAL
**Reason For Joining Baywatch:** Apparently there wasn't enough action for him in the Navy. After all, only lifeguards get to fight terrorists and drug-smugglers.
**Line of Dialogue That Best Sums Up His Character:** 'Gotta seize the moment, cookie.'
**Self Confidence as Expressed Through a Food Analogy:** 'Why should she settle for hamburger like you when she can have steak like me?'
**Best Reason for Beating Someone Up:** To teach him the importance of working with children
**Percentage of His Clothing That Was Fashionable in the Early Eighties:** 95%
**Number of Times That He's Demonstrated Superhuman Strength:** 5
**Number of Times He's Been Able To Stop Armed Bad Guys by Beating Them Up:** 14
**Biggest Complaint About Being a Lifeguard:** 'The pay stinks.'
**Proof He's Lying:** He owns a huge house and a Jeep Cherokee, and he can afford a housemaid
**Number of Times He's Made References to David Hasselhoff's Career:** 4
**Number of Pictures of Himself on His Mantelpiece:** 4
**Number of Times That He's Been Suspicious of the Intentions of Fat Guys:** 4
**Number of Times That Men Have Tried to Kill Him Because He's Too Attractive:** 3
**Most Inexplicable Lie Told to a Child:** The ocean takes your footprints to Hawaii
**Number of Times He's Cried Like a Sissy-Boy:** 7
**Most Disturbing Similarity Between Mitch and God:** In 'Hot Stuff,' Mitch speaks to Hobie from a burning bush

*These guys are up to no good.*

# Adept Lifeguard or SUPERHERO?

Mitch has the remarkable ability to survive any sort of disaster, no matter how perilous. How does he do it? His years of lifeguarding have taught him a number of innovative survival skills that have helped him deal with even the most life-threatening situations. Some examples:

### DANGER
Shark in the water.

### SOLUTION
Grab some driftwood and beat it up.

### DANGER
Serial killer is holding two lifeguards hostage in a beach tower.

### SOLUTION
Tunnel under the sand like Bugs Bunny, then beat him up.

## DANGER
Bad Hawaiians are chasing you with spears.

## SOLUTION
Put shirt in bush to distract them, then beat them up.

## DANGER
You suspect that a basketball player has been involved in murder.

## SOLUTION
Beat him in a basketball game, then beat him up.

## DANGER
A swarthy man is stalking your son and his friend.

## SOLUTION
Chase him in a truck, then let midgets beat him up.

*Ready to kick ass for Mitch!*

17

# C.J. PARKER

In the opening of 'The Life You Save,' children of every race and creed are playing together on the beach. They run and laugh, holding hands and throwing flowers. They have learned to live together in perfect harmony, and watching over them is C.J. Parker, dressed in a flowing white dress and smiling like an approving goddess. The children rush over and embrace her, and C.J. laughs, holding her loyal and beautiful children close to her bosom.

Meet C.J. Parker. She's more than just a bodacious blonde bombshell with a heart of gold. She may very well be the Weeping Madonna of Southern California.

# Raw Data

**Sex:** Female

**Age:** 23

**Age Five Years From Now:** 23

**Interests:** New Age philosophy, environmentalism, fashion, gambling

**Interests That Involve Wearing Skimpy or Tight-fitting Outfits:** All of above

**Most Amazing Attributes:** Water-resistant makeup, ability to heal facial scars within seconds

**Average Number of Lives Saved Per Episode:** 0.64

**Average Number of Romances With Men Per Episode:** 1.56

**Average Number of Gratuitous Boob Shots Per Episode:** 3

*Three per episode.*

**Average Percentage of Her Dialogue That Doesn't Involve Verbs:** 35%

**Average Percentage of Screen Time That Involves Running in Slow Motion:** 68%

**Best Pick-Up Line Used On Her:** 'But *I'm* drowning. Drowning in your love.'

**Percentage of Suitors Who Are Fat and Ugly:** 76%

**Percentage of Fat and Ugly Suitors That She Has Turned Down:** 100%

**Total Number of Times She's Had Sex:** 0

**Total Number of Times She's Kissed a Man:** 23

**Total Number of Times She's Had Tickle Fights:** 3

**Most Frequently Used Expressions of True Love**

  **For a Man:** Walking on the beach with him, running on the beach with him, standing on the beach with him, tickle fights

*Too fat, too ugly.*

# Pam Anderson Lee
## *Fun Facts*

**Thoughts on *Baywatch* character:** 'She's a real hippy-dippy, just like me.'

**Career Prior to *Baywatch*:** Labatt's beer poster girl, Home Improvement's tool girl, *Playboy* magazine's nudie girl

**Most Impressive Awards:** Worst Dressed, 1995, *People* magazine; Playmate of the Month, 1990, *Playboy* magazine

**Best Scandal:** Melissa Parks, her stand-in on *Baywatch*, told *American Journal* in 1995 that Pam's breasts are fake

**Her Response to Accusations of Plastic Surgery:** 'I've only had a little, not enough to notice.'

**Proof Positive That She Is Lying:** 1990 Blue Zone ad for Labatt's Beer

**Estimated Number of Pictures of Pam on the World Wide Web:** 1048

**Estimated Number of Pictures of Pam on the Web in Which She is Naked:** 769

**Married To:** Tommy Lee, Motley Crüe drummer, for one year and counting

**Husband's Most Dubious Claim About Relationship:** 'Sex has nothing to do with it.'

**Couple's Favorite Extra-Curricular Activity:** Pam swings naked over Tommy's piano while he composes heavy metal songs

**Royal Recognition:** Peter Phillips, the grandson of the Queen and Duke of Edinburgh, refused to take down his pin-ups of Pam in his dorm-room at Gordonstoun

20

# Beware the Bay Siren

C.J. has a way of attracting every man on the beach. Although it's easy to understand the temptation, most of her suitors end up suffering from personal tragedy shortly after meeting her. Is C.J. the perfect woman, or a siren who lures men to destruction? Here is a list of some of the men who have loved C.J., and whose lives she has ravished:

**John D. Cort** — Loses eyesight

**Carlton** — Falls off cliff

**Karl** — Killed by an escaped convict, then dumped into ocean

**Angelo** — Lost dance contest

**Maroni the Magnificent** — Nearly drowns during a bungled underwater stunt

**Father Ryan** — Loses faith and almost gives up priesthood

**Craig the Marine Biologist** — Busted for jewel-smuggling

# The Many Moods of Matt

Matt Brody has proven to be one of the most emotionally complex characters on *Baywatch*. Not since Hamlet has there been a character of such depth and magnitude. If you don't believe us, just take a look at this retrospective of some of Matt's most memorable emoting. We ask you, with acting like this, who needs character development?

## 1. ANGRY
Uh-oh. Better back off! Matt's pissed off and looking for trouble.

## 2. SAD
Poor ol' Matt. He's in a poo-poo mood. Somebody needs a hug.

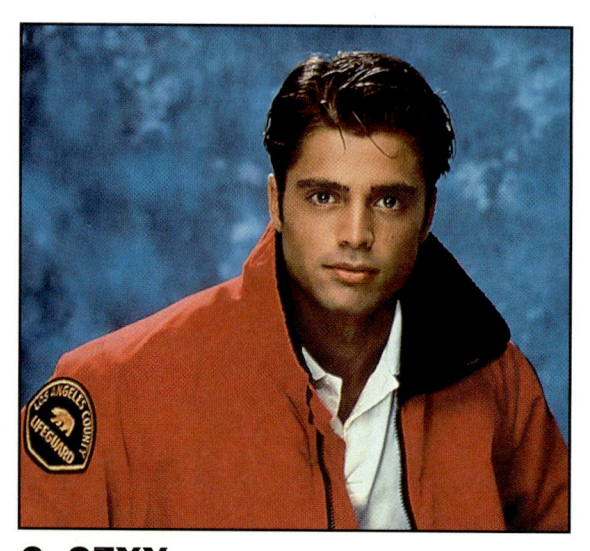

## 3. SEXY
Hello ladies! Look into Matt's eyes and you'll know he's ready for love.

## 4. INTROSPECTIVE
When the world gets too complicated for Matt, he likes to tune out for a while.

# Stephanie Holden

In 'Rookie of the Year,' Stephanie Holden instructed a group of young lifeguards-in-training. She introduced them to the rescue can, which she described as 'your life's blood.' She made it perfectly clear that she was the master and they only lowly pupils. 'There's not one of you I can't totally dominate in the water,' she said. 'Not one of you who could threaten my life with mere strength.'

When Matt Brody showed up late, she punished him by using him as an example. She punched him in the gut with her rescue can, threw him into the pool and then almost drowned him. When Mitch asked her to lay off, she reminded him that 'Our job is to weed out the ones who don't have what it takes.'

Later that same day, she did some paperwork.

Thus is the sublime dualism of Stephanie Holden. She is both hard-nosed leader and paper-pushing secretary. She kicks ass, and then she cleans up after herself. She destroys the souls of men, and then she files them in alphabetical order. Stephanie rules the beach with an iron fist, and makes sure that everything is perfectly organized. She is pretty much the perfect lifeguard, except for one fatal flaw that continues to haunt her to this day.

She has really, really small breasts.

'I am *holding my breath.*'

# Raw Data

**Sex:** Female
**Age:** 29
**Reason For Joining *Baywatch*:** She cares about people
**Real Reason For Joining *Baywatch*:** She's in the market for a husband
**Biggest Assets As a Lifeguard:** Likes to intimidate young boys; tiny wrists make it easy for her to slip out of handcuffs
**Line That Best Sums Up Her Character:** 'I have some paperwork to do, so get outta here!'
**Interests:** Environmental concerns, saving the planet, having a baby
**Average Percentage of Screen Time That Involves Doing Paperwork:** 15%
**Defining Characteristics:** Big teeth, tiny breasts, skin cancer
**Number of Times That She's Made People Stop Having Fun:** 14
**Number of Times That She's Been the 'Rational One':** 11
**Number of Times That Her Sister Has Accused Her of Playing Mom:** 6
**Number of Times That Other Characters Have Accused Her of Playing Mom:** 2
**Favorite Type of Man:** Boat-owning, facial hair-growing, earth-hugging, humorless environmentalists
**Main Irony of Her Career:** Having survived gunfire, explosives, shark attacks, drowning and murderous psychopaths, she's finally been done in by a cancerous mole

*'There's not one of you I can't totally dominate in the water.'*

*'You'll feel better after a good workout.'*

When anyone at *Baywatch* has a problem, they usually go to Stephanie for advice and guidance. She just seems to know more about life and how to make sense of it than any other lifeguard on the beach. It made us wonder if Stephanie would ever consider starting her own advice column. Surely the rest of us could stand to learn a thing or two from her wise counsel. We took some random quotes from her many deliberations with troubled lifeguards and used them to create the very first 'Dear Stephanie' column. Maybe someday she will find the time to answer all of our questions, and then the healing can finally begin.

As Stephanie would say, 'You'll feel better after a good workout.' And we couldn't agree more.

# Dear Stephanie

**Good Advice From the *Baywatch* Den Mother**

---

Dear Stephanie,
I want to be a lifeguard because I think it'd be a great way to meet some gorgeous babes. Is it ethical for a lifeguard to use CPR as an excuse to kiss somebody?

Horny Lifesaver

---

Dear Horny Lifesaver,
Mister, mouth-to-mouth resuscitation is not kissing. A lifeguard may have to give mouth-to-mouth to a two-hundred-and-fifty-pound truck driver or a three-year-old child. It is not a situation where one chooses a partner. This is not the Dating Game. Is that clear?

---

Dear Stephanie,
I recently found out that the guy I've been dating is married. I was upset at first, but I still want to continue dating him. I'm so confused. I don't know what's right or wrong anymore. Can you help me?

Novice Mistress

---

Dear Novice Mistress,
You were involved in a traumatic situation. What you're feeling, what you're going through, has got a name. It's called Critical Incident Stress. You can't believe it's your fault. I know how you must feel, but you did the right thing. You can't count on a relationship with a married man, unless you're the one married to him. In a way, I envy you. I envy your ability to follow your instincts, regardless of what logic dictates. You go for it, the hurt be damned. I'm not trusting enough. For once, I wish that I could just be able to fall in love without analyzing the relationship.

# Logan Fowler

Nobody likes Logan Fowler, and with good reason. As fellow lifeguard Matt Brody describes him, 'He's lazy, reckless, irresponsible and you can't believe a word he says.' In less than two years with the *Baywatch* team, he has managed to double-cross, betray or nearly kill almost every character on the show. Even worse, he has shown no sign that he regrets his actions, or has any intention of changing. In fact, he seems to revel in his bad-boy image.

But there is more to Logan than his so-called 'hotdog tactics.' He does have a heart, although it is difficult to find. When he first came to *Baywatch*, he started making trouble almost immediately. He threatened Matt with violence, condescended to Stephanie and C.J., nearly killed a fellow lifeguard in a rescue attempt, and flirted with Caroline while she was still married. But when he became rookie of the year and was allowed to choose the beach he wanted to work at, he chose *Baywatch*, even knowing that everybody there hated him. 'After all we've been through together,' he said to the group, 'I feel very close to you all. You're like my family.'

Sure, Logan is a jerk. But he's a jerk with a big heart. Like a parent spanking his child, he's only doing it because he loves us.

# Raw Data

**Sex:** Male

**Age:** 22

**Reason For Joining Baywatch:**
'I want to save lives.'

**Real Reason For Joining Baywatch:**
'I intend to find a rich, beautiful Malibu woman who'll take care of my every need. This is the land of opportunity.'

**Interests:** 'Rubber Ducky' racing, sleeping with his friends' girlfriends

**Line of Dialogue That Best Sums Up His Character:** 'You got a problem with me? Let's settle it right here.'

**Number of Gratuitous Ass or Pec Shots in a Typical Season:** 18

**Percentage of His Dialogue That's Sarcastic:** 86%

**Number of Times That He's Disregarded Orders:** 12

**Number of Lives That He's Saved:** 15

**Number of Lives That He's Saved When the Victim Just So Happened to Be a Beautiful Woman or a Rich Widow:** 13

**Reason For Dating a Woman:** She's involved with somebody else

**Reason For Marrying a Woman:** She's rich

**Biggest Lie:** 'I don't hurt other people to get what I want.'

**Best Rationale For Bad-Boy Behavior:** 'I've been having nightmares.'

# Caroline Holden

In 'Rubber Ducky,' Caroline Holden fantasizes about her true love, Logan Fowler, a man that she can never really have to herself. In her vision of paradise, she and Logan run along the beach and look meaningfully into each other's eyes. Then they do sit-ups. She holds his feet as he pumps his stomach muscles into submission, and then he holds her feet as she shows him what she's got. She falls back from the workout, her face sweaty and contorted in ecstasy. This, for her, is the way things should be. One man. One woman. Two hundred ab crunches.

Caroline's dream of perfect love may not always make much sense, but neither does anything in her troubled life. She is a woman who sometimes seems to exist only to endure pain. But we must trust that there is a method to her madness. Perhaps she is a pioneer of sorts, embodying the fearless journey that we must all take towards self-discovery and emancipation. She could be an icon of our times, a symbol of courage and determination. If she can succeed, than perhaps the meek shall one day inherit the earth.

Either that, or she's just some crazy chick who gets beaten up a lot. Either way.

# Raw Data

- **Sex:** Female
  **Age:** 21
  **Line That Best Sums Up Her Character:** 'Why does every guy I meet think that I'm their personal punching bag?'
  **Interests:** Dating Australian men, being abused by boyfriends, crying
- **Favorite Type of Victim:** Disabled sports legends
  **Average Percentage of Screen Time Spent Pouting and/or Crying:** 89%
  **Number of Times That She's Had Sex:** 0
  **Number of Times That She's Thought She Was Pregnant:** 1
  **Percentage of Boyfriends Who've Betrayed Her:** 75%
  **Percentage of Suitors Who Have Held Her at Gun-point or Taken Her Hostage:** 25%
- **Fantasy Life:** Dreams of being on *Charlie's Angels*, dreams of being with boyfriends who don't abuse her

# Whoops!
## Caroline's Guide To Crisis Management

No one on *Baywatch* screws up as much as Caroline. She's botched more than a few rescues in her time, and her incompetence has resulted in the only dead drowning victim in the show's history. Few of us could handle the pressures of being responsible for so much damage, but somehow Caroline manages to survive it all. Here are just a few of her methods for overcoming the guilt of a blundering lifestyle.

**Crisis**
A drunk college guy drowned because you weren't paying attention during a rescue.

**Solution**
Wear lots of leather, start drinking heavily, date a biker thug and weep constantly.

**Crisis**
A young boy nearly drowned because you were watching Logan flirt with some girls.

**Solution**
Complain to your sister that you can't work on the same beach as Logan, then accuse her of butting into your business when she tries to transfer him to another beach.

**Crisis**
A man with AIDS tries to drown himself and blames you for saving him.

**Solution**
Cook some lasagna, then weep (the pouting is optional).

*At last, Logan's mine*

*Look at the love bumpers on that!*

# BAYWATCH EPISODE GUIDE (ABRIDGED)

If you were stranded on a deserted island and could have only five episodes of *Baywatch* for entertainment, which five would you choose? Luckily, few of us will ever have to face this dilemma, as *Baywatch* is so heavily broadcast that you'd probably be able to find it on even the most remote atoll in Micronesia, but it does bring up an interesting point. What are the five *best* episodes of *Baywatch*?

To answer this question, we conducted extensive research of the existing *Baywatch* repertoire in order to determine what constitutes a truly excellent episode. Using the information we gathered in our studies, we created a strict and complex series of criteria which we used to judge the entries in our competition. For instance, can the plot of a particular episode be summarized in ten words or less? If it cannot, then it is too complicated to be considered 'classic' *Baywatch* and is disqualified from the running. Episodes were also judged on their use of serious scenes that are unintentionally funny, and their creativity in justifying their flagrant displays of tits and ass.

We believe that these five episodes represent the best that *Baywatch* has to offer, and deserve to be included in the canon of twentieth-century arts and literature. Or, at the very least, they're worth taping and keeping on a shelf at home.

**THE 5 BEST**

# 1. Vacation

(*Season 3*)
Rating: 🔴 🔴 🔴 🔴

**Synopsis in Ten Words or Less:** Lifeguards take vacation cruise, but don't get to relax.
**What Sets It Apart From Other Episodes:** It has a refreshingly cynical perspective on love for such a usually pro-love show. All three of the romances in this two-parter end in disaster. The frustrated lovers are inflicted with huge gambling debts, chased by fat and unattractive widows, or thrown into the ocean to die.
**Absurd Yet Poignant Moment:** Stephanie tells Mitch that she loves him just as they are about to be eaten by sharks.
**Creative Excuse For Showing Lots of Flesh:** The lifeguards are on vacation, so they get to wear a lot of skimpy bikinis instead of those form-fitting lifeguard uniforms.
**Why It Stands Up To Repeated Viewing:** Almost every plot point reaches glorious heights of implausibility. Mitch and Stephanie fall into the ocean, lose their life preserver, fight off the waves, hypothermia and shark attacks, and *don't die*. Some gangsters have hijacked the cruise ship, and even though they have guns and muscle on their side, *Matt and Summer stop them*. Guido tries to seduce a woman *and succeeds*.

# 2. Silent Night, Baywatch Night

(*Season 5*)
Rating: 🔴🔴🔴🔴

**Synopsis in Ten Words or Less:** Small people of every age make Christmas at *Baywatch* special.

**What Sets It Apart From Other Episodes:** *Baywatch* has never been more bizarre. Matt befriends a group of egotistical midgets. Mitch lets a runaway girl sleep in his bed. C.J. seduces a priest. Mitch falls in love with a cancerous woman. There may be no snow during Christmas in California, but there is plenty of questionable activity.

**Absurd Yet Poignant Moment:** Matt discovers that one of the midgets has been hiding Christmas presents at the *Baywatch* headquarters. Caught red-handed, the midget admits that he works for Santa Claus and lives in the North Pole. Matt believes him.

**Creative Excuse For Showing Lots of Flesh:** The midgets do a lot of sunbathing and swimming, and wear very revealing swimsuits. At times, it feels uncomfortably like child pornography.

**Why It Stands Up To Repeated Viewing:** Who could grow tired of all them midgets?

*There may be no snow during Christmas in California but there is plenty of questionable activity.*

*There's a lot of belly-dancing in Hawaii.*

*Lifeguards go to Hawaii and steal their women.*

# 3. Forbidden Paradise

(*Season 6*)
Rating: 🛟 🛟 🛟

**Synopsis in Ten Words or Less:** Lifeguards go to Hawaii and steal their women.
**What Sets It Apart From Other Episodes:** *Baywatch* has had its fair share of zany ethnic men being chased by white people, but in this episode, zany ethnic men are *chasing* white people.
**Absurd Yet Poignant Moment:** On a boat outing, Matt is stung by a poisonous scorpionfish. Mitch drags him through the jungle, but Matt grows weaker and weaker. Matt finally asks Mitch to go on without him. But Mitch refuses and, in the ultimate act of friendship, pushes him off a cliff, into a river.
**Creative Excuse For Showing Lots of Flesh:** There's a *lot* of belly-dancing in Hawaii.
**Why It Stands Up To Repeated Viewing:** This episode was originally released as a straight-to-video film, so you can rent it any damn time you want. That's enough of a reason right there.

# 4. Red Wind

(*Season 5*)
Rating: 🔴 🔴 🔴 🔴

**Synopsis in Ten Words or Less:** Everybody on the beach is horny.

**What Sets It Apart From Other Episodes:** The 'special' guest star is Geraldo Rivera, an American talk show personality. Although he is not an actor, he somehow manages to act circles around the rest of the cast.

**Absurd Yet Poignant Moment:** A group of New Agers choose C.J. as their spiritual leader after a tarot card is blown by the wind on to her gigantic bosoms.

**Creative Excuse For Showing Lots of Flesh:** Those darn Santa Ana winds are making all the girls take off their bikinis and flash the male lifeguards.

**Why It Stands Up To Repeated Viewing:** It can't decide what it wants to be. Is it a sex farce? Is it a tragedy? Caroline feels bad that a child has drowned. C.J. tries to make people stop screwing on the beach. Caroline visits the child's father in the hospital and cries. A sexy woman chases Mitch around the beach and tries to grab his butt. It's like getting six different episodes for the price of one.

# 5. Baywatch Angels

(*Season 6*)
Rating: 🔴 🔴 🔴

**Synopsis in Ten Words or Less:** Caroline fantasizes about *Charlie's Angels* and then saves Logan's life.

**What Sets It Apart From Other Episodes:** Unlike 'Rescue Bay,' which was a TV show within a TV show, this is a TV show that *becomes* another TV show.

**Absurd Yet Poignant Moment:** The *Baywatch* Angels meet the *Baywatch* lifeguards, and discover that they *both* have really big hair

**Creative Excuse For Showing Lots of Flesh:** If you remember, the original Charlie's Angels wore a lot of tight clothes. And so, in keeping with this tradition, the *Baywatch* Angels do the same. Hey, what choice did they have?

**Why It Stands Up To Repeated Viewing:** The more you watch it, the more you realize that there really isn't much difference between the two shows.

35

# BAYWATCH LIFEGUARD MANUAL

In the world of *Baywatch*, there are only two types of people: a lifeguard and an *anti*-lifeguard. You are either a strong and noble leader of the people, or you are some weak vermin who needs to be saved or crushed at all costs. But in the coming new world order, when *Baywatch* finally has complete political and social control of the planet, you will have to decide what your role will be in the new empire. Are you a lifeguard or an *enemy* of the lifeguard? To put it another way, are you on the side of Good, or are you going to give in to the temptations of the Dark Side? The choice is up to you.

If you decide that you want to be a lifeguard, you should begin familiarizing yourself with the basics. To aid you in the process, we've put together a beginner's guide to lifeguard training. Follow it closely, study hard, and God save your soul.

## Do You Have What it Takes to be a BAYWATCH Lifeguard?

The first mistake that most would-be lifeguards make is assuming that the only requirement is a working knowledge of CPR and other life-saving tactics. This is not true. In order to become a bona fide *Baywatch* lifeguard, you must possess a very specific type of personality. Anyone can learn how to drag a drowning boy out of the water, but only a real *Baywatch* lifeguard has the instinct to know that the boy is probably part of a jewel-smuggling racket, and that the only way to stop it is to seduce the boy's mother and then chase gangsters on the beach in a long and complicated montage.

If you think that you fit this personality type, take this test and find out for certain ...

1. **Which of the following best describes you?**
   a. A buxom blonde with a heart of gold and a tendency to run in slow motion
   b. A beefy stud-muffin with a bad attitude who just needs to be loved
   c. A confused teenager who loves to surf but needs life-guidance
   d. A zany ethnic stereotype who wears ill-fitting clothes and gets into all kinds of crazy misadventures

   *'Is that a rescue can or are you just glad to see me?'*

2. **When did you know that you wanted to be a lifeguard?**
   a. Realized that you were afraid of sharks, drowning, diving, speedboats, or anything water-related
   b. Spouse divorced you, had nothing better to do
   c. Majority of life occurs in montages
   d. Wife left you because you weren't 'as cool' as Mitch Buchannon

3. **What is the biggest danger that can befall a swimmer at the beach?**
   a. World War II mines!
   b. They're held hostage by jewel thieves/ murderers/ escaped mental patients
   c. Lifeguards are so attractive and brave that visiting civilians can't help but be consumed with lust and desire
   d. They could meet a rich widow and have thoughts of leaving their girlfriend

   *'It's another one of those damn World War II mines!'*

37

4. What would you describe as your chief disappointment and/or frustration in life?
   a. Brother's nickname was 'Buzzy'
   b. Have yet to achieve D cup
   c. Insistence that you are the 'Rubber Ducky' champ fails to impress the babes
   d. Traumatic flashbacks usually accompanied by David Hasselhoff songs

*Stephanie dreams of achieving a D cup.*

5. How would you define 'teamwork'?
   a. Do not run over fellow lifeguard with a speedboat in order to save a drowning woman, even if she is attractive
   b. Cover shift for fellow lifeguard when his girlfriend is dying from cancer
   c. If a crazy ethnic stereotype is chasing one lifeguard, he is chasing all lifeguards
   d. If fellow lifeguard has been sucked into underwater cavern, save him

6. What has been your experience with love and romance?
   a. Everyone you fall for either dies of some horrible disease or divorces you
   b. Everyone you fall for turns out to be a criminal or a priest
   c. You only date lifeguards, preferably somebody who is already involved with another lifeguard
   d. You tend to attract homely, overweight widows, who chase you around the beach and make high-pitched yelping noises

*Everyone you fall for turns out to be a criminal or a priest.*

38

7. How would you describe your relationship with your father?
   a. Father never wanted you to be a lifeguard, because he's a rich old bastard
   b. Father never wanted you to be a lifeguard, and now he's dead
   c. Father was too busy being a compulsive gambler and womanizer to notice that you wanted to be a lifeguard
   d. Dad was a lifeguard, so he approved of your career choice. But he died in a tragic boat rescue, making you wonder if you shouldn't be a lifeguard.

*Do you have what it takes to become a Baywatch lifeguard?*

8. If you couldn't be a lifeguard, what other career would you pursue?
   a. Fashion model and Greenpeace volunteer
   b. Surfing champ and calendar model
   c. Bulimic
   d. Private detective, with zany ethnic stereotype as your partner

# How to Talk Like a
# *Lifeguardin' Dude*

To be a successful Baywatcher, you have to be able to talk the talk. But conversing like a bona fide California lifeguard is not as simple as knowing the difference between a rip current and an undertow. You also need to become well-versed in some of the more 'bitchin'' terminology. Here are a few examples from the dictionary of Lifeguard Lingo, taken from the official '*Baywatch* Writers' Bible.'

- **Beat-off:** an untrustworthy lifeguard
- **Bogus:** phony, weird
- **Bud:** one of the guys
- **Buffasorus:** one who is in shape and 'looking good'
- **Cruiser:** a pick-up artist, usually male
- **Dirt bag:** bum
- **Patrol:** walk
- **Fluff and Buff:** to get ready, shave and shower

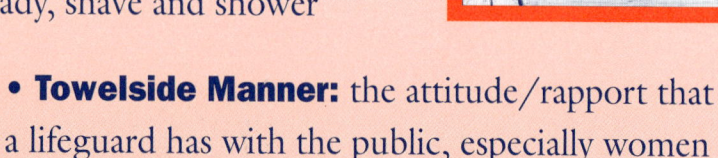

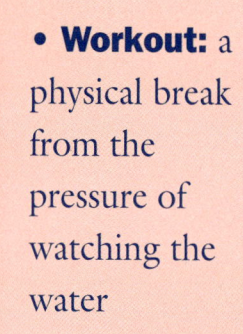

*What a buffasorus!*

- **Towelside Manner:** the attitude/rapport that a lifeguard has with the public, especially women

- **Workout:** a physical break from the pressure of watching the water

**Towelside Manner**

**Workout**

# LIFEGUARDS EN MASSE

One of the most important lessons that a *Baywatch* lifeguard must learn is that he is not alone. In 'Red Wind,' it took eight lifeguards to rescue one small child. If we assume the kid weighed between 60 to 80 pounds, that means that there is approximately one lifeguard for every 8.75 drowning pounds. Using this equation, we calculated how many lifeguards would be necessary for bigger, more weighty disasters:

### A kid
(Total weight of 72 pounds):
8.37 lifeguards

### A full-grown man
(Total weight of 193 pounds):
22 lifeguards

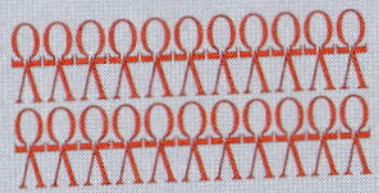

### Family of four
(Total weight of 470 pounds):
53.71 lifeguards

### Family of four and car
(Total weight of 1,380 pounds):
157.7 lifeguards

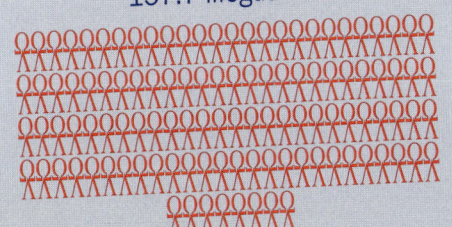

### Whale
(Total weight of four tons): 1,024 lifeguards

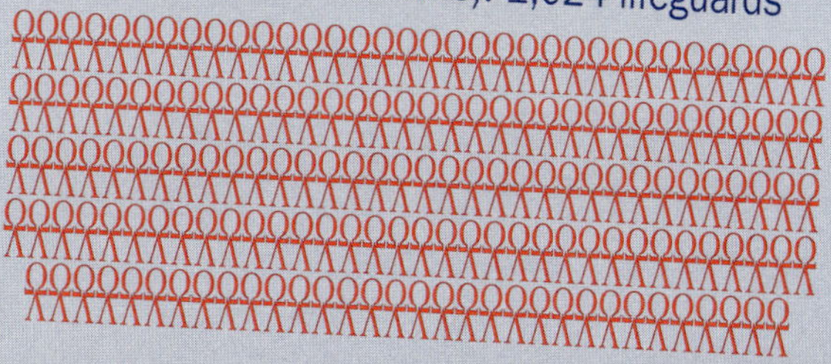

# THE PLANET

*Stephanie Holden*

*Caroline Holden*

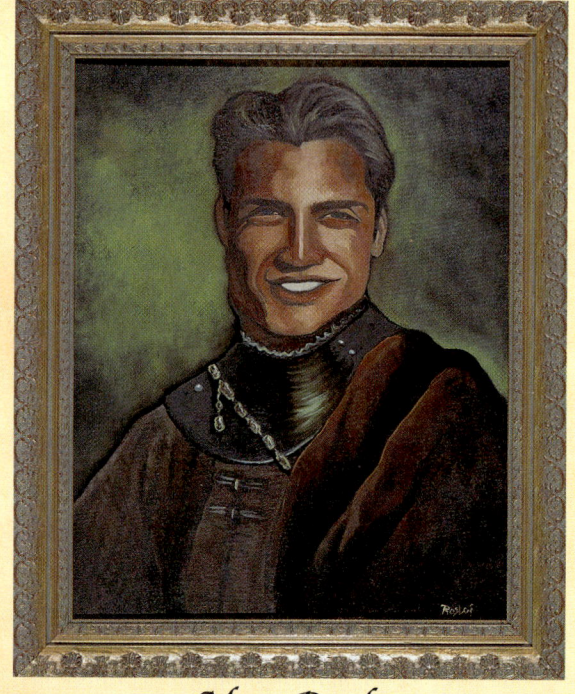

*Matt Brody*

*Logan Fowler*

# Baywatch Room

## At The National Portrait Gallery, London, England

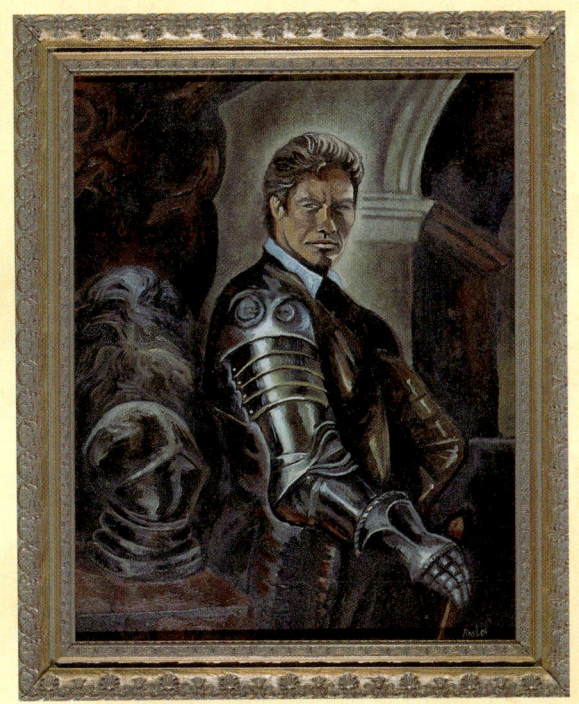

Mitch Buchannon

Hobie Buchannon

Neely Capshaw and Cody Madison

# Water-Related Injuries Only *Please*

A show about lifeguards is, by definition, limited in its plot possibilities. After all, a lifeguard is only qualified to save people who are drowning. What happens when you run out of interesting conflicts that take place in water? Simple. You bring the water *to* the conflict.

**HE CAN'T SWIM**

*I'M DROWNING! HELP!*

### Dry-land Plotline
Matt challenges a murderous hoodlum to a motorcycle race.

### But then ...
The hoodlum skids off the road and into the bay. He can't swim.

### Dry-land Plotline
Hobie takes a trip on a private jet with Mitch's ex-wife and her rich fiancé.

### But then ...
The plane crashes into the ocean. None of them can swim.

**SHE CAN'T SWIM**

**Dry-land Plotline**
Mitch and a visiting FBI agent spy on some gangsters.

**But then...**
Inexplicably, one of the gangsters decides to go into the water. She can't swim.

**Dry-land Plotline**
Teenage punks crash Matt's party and do a lot of drugs.

**But then...**
They fall into the pool, and because they're high on drugs, they can't swim.

**Dry-land Plotline**
A group of UFO enthusiasts visit the beach in hopes of meeting aliens.

**But then...**
Thinking that the aliens are in the water, they all run in to meet them. There are no aliens, and none of them can swim.

**NONE OF THEM CAN SWIM**

**Dry-land Plotline**
On a luxurious cruise ship, Lt. Stephanie Holden stumbles into the middle of a mafia assassination.

**But then...**
While attempting to get away, Stephanie falls off the ship. Although she is a lifeguard, she cannot swim.

45

# An Introduction to
# The Montage

## *If you Can't Talk about it, Point to it*

To truly appreciate the aesthetics of *Baywatch*, you must possess a working knowledge of the montage. Building on the grand traditions of musical theater, the *Baywatch* Montage combines pop music and slo-mo jiggling to convey character development without using up valuable words. It has become such an essential ingredient in the *Baywatch* equation that to disregard it is to miss the entire beauty of the show.

Think of it this way: in most episodes of *Baywatch*, the montages make up almost one quarter of the show. It could be argued that the montage does not serve the show, but rather the show serves the montage.

*Slo-mo jiggling is essential to convey character development.*

## How To Identify a Montage

Many first-time *Baywatch* viewers have difficulty spotting a montage when they see it. To aid you in your *Baywatch* studies, here are some of the signs that will alert you to the presence of a bona fide montage.

## 1. Nothing is happening

Does it seem to you that the entire plot has come to a standstill, that you've been given information that could have been more easily explained in a sentence or two? Is there a repetition of one simple event, or even no event, such as a lifeguard staring at the water? If so, you are probably watching a montage.

## 2. Everybody is running in slow motion

Although slow-motion running occurs throughout the show, it is a dominant theme in the montage. Whether a casual jog or a high-speed chase, everybody is running and taking their own sweet time about it.

*If it seems like you're watching a bad student film that's trying too hard to look surreal and experimental, then you're probably watching a montage.*

Perhaps it's because the writers want us to appreciate just how much effort goes into running and they'd like us to pause and appreciate all the subtle qualities of a lifeguard in motion. Whatever the logic, if you see a character running in slow motion for over two minutes, you can be fairly confident that you're watching a montage.

## 3. David Hasselhoff is making a funny face

David Hasselhoff is the master of the funny face, and nowhere does he practice his craft more than in the montage. But it's not just Hasselhoff; almost every actor on *Baywatch* has, at one time or another, used the montage to demonstrate their funny face abilities.

*Hasselhoff: master of the funny face.*

## 4. There's lots of 'arty' editing

If the picture fluctuates wildly between black-and-white and color, if the editing is so fast and furious that it makes you dizzy and nauseous, if it seems like you're watching a bad student film that's trying too hard to look surreal and experimental, then you're probably watching a montage.

*Pop ditties used in montages are hardly ever appropriate.*

## 5. The accompanying song doesn't fit the mood

During most of the show, the background music makes sense in relation to the action taking place. But for some reason, the pop ditties used in montages are hardly ever appropriate. For example, in a montage involving two lifeguards saving a child, the accompanying song is 'Do the Funky Junkie.'

## 6. It looks like an episode of *Benny Hill*

A woman drops her towel and is gawked at by double-taking buffoons. A short and balding old man is shoved to the ground and laughed at by attractive, smirking studs. An overweight man is being chased by boobacious women in bikinis. If you see any of the above and you think to yourself, 'Wait a minute, I thought we were watching *Baywatch*. Who turned on *Benny Hill*?' then you have definitely spotted a montage.

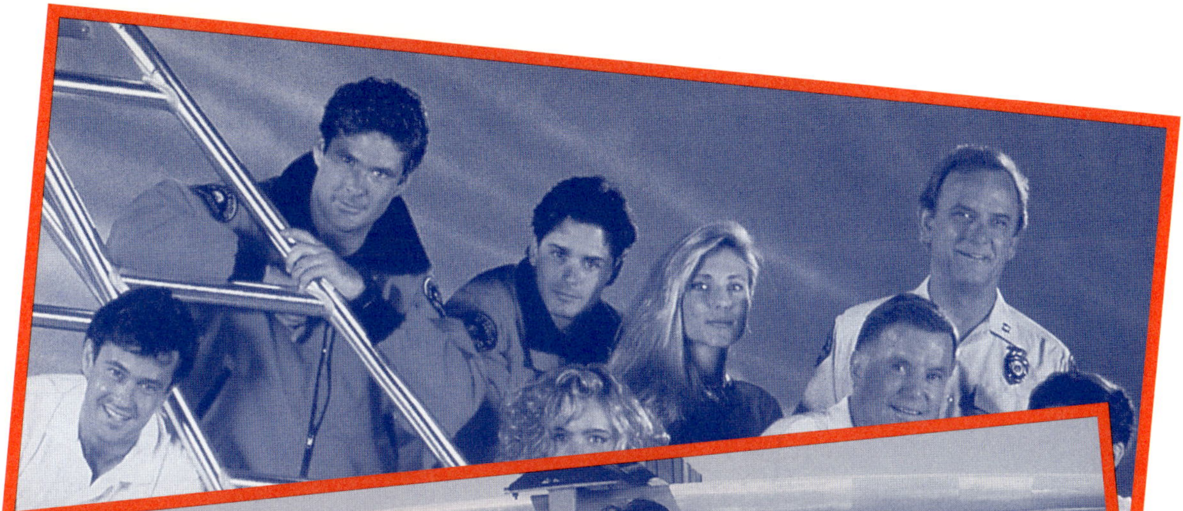

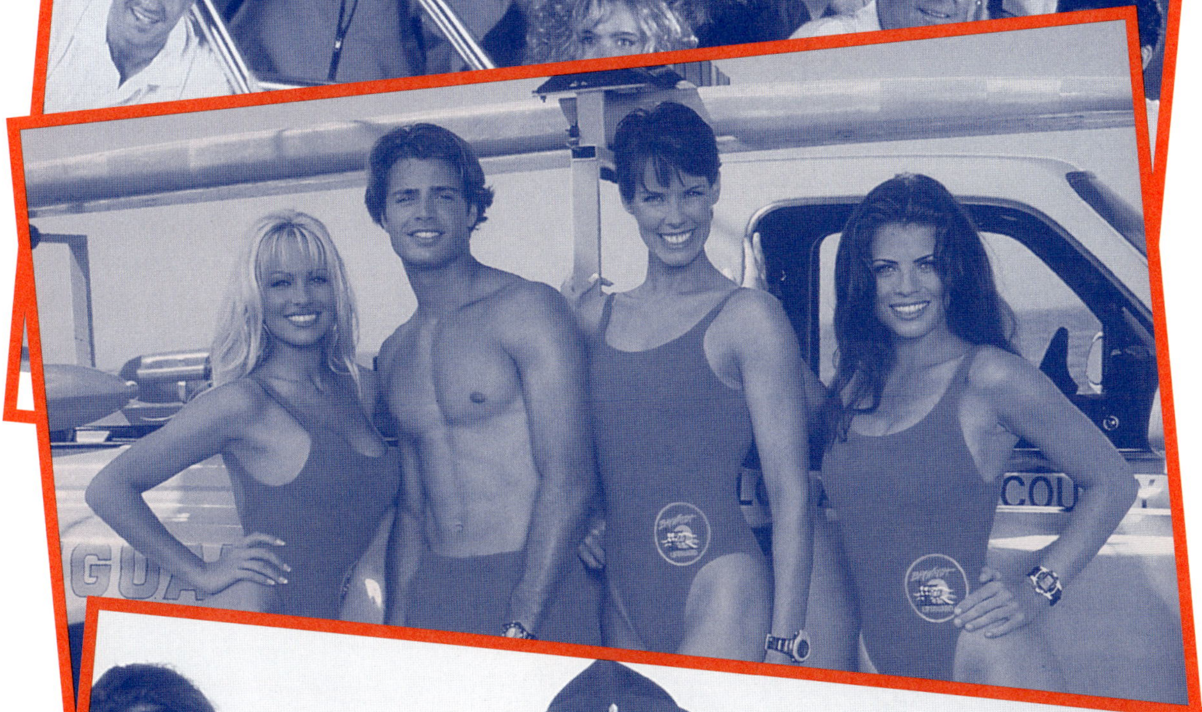

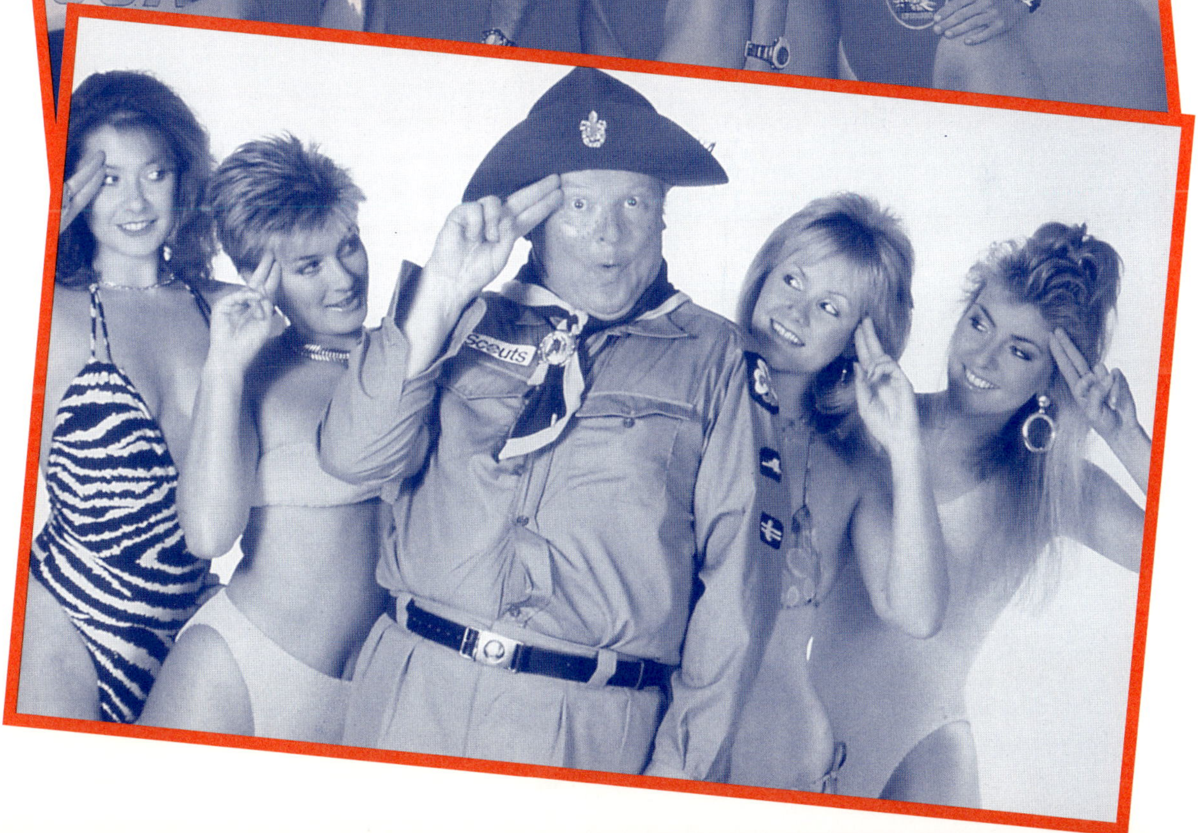

## THE MONTAGE GLOSSARY

# The We're Falling in Love Montage

There are many ways to fall in love on *Baywatch*, but most often people fall in love in montages. Love is, after all, a very complex thing, and words can't always express emotions as eloquently as the image of two young lovers running towards each other in slow motion while a top-40 pop song plays in the background.

As the Love Montage teaches us, there is no better place to fall in love than the beach. Sometimes just *being* on the beach

*Water is an essential ingredient in the act of falling in love.*

is enough to bring about true love. In 'Baja Run,' C.J. and Matt are walking on the beach, feeling bad about being dumped by their respective beaus. They see each other, start running and then, in a matter of seconds, start kissing passionately in the surf. All told, it takes them a grand total of three minutes and twenty seconds to fall in love. Apparently the beach acts as a sort of aphrodisiac, with such a complete control over our emotional lives that we are powerless to resist.

*Sometimes just being on the beach is enough to bring about true love.*

50

# THE MONTAGE GLOSSARY

*High on life . . . and each other!*

But more so than the beach, water is an essential ingredient in the act of falling in love. In 'Seize the Day,' Tracy and Mitch eat lunch at a gazebo (who can resist the erotic siren song of the gazebo?), and then, to top off a splendid evening, splash each other with water. In 'Tower of Power,' Stephanie dances with an attractive ethnic lifeguard in the rain. Eventually they run into the ocean and splash each other with water. In 'Tequila Bay,' Summer watches Slade surf and falls in love with him. Then she surfs with him and, in the ultimate act of love, splashes him with water. One can't help but wonder if this is some kind of baptizing ritual, as if the other person must be 'purified' before being accepted into the gospel of love.

For those characters not keen on getting wet, you can also fall in love by playing recreational sports with your prospective lover. In 'Lover's Cove,' Matt and Summer fall in love after a montage of running in the park, playing hide-and-seek and one-on-one basketball. Later in the same episode, Hobie wins the heart of a young girl when he takes her for a ride on a wave-runner.

The Love Montage can do more than show how people fall in love, it can also show how love can fall apart. In 'Guys & Dolls,' Stephanie and her new boyfriend eat lunch in the park, play basketball and then walk on the beach. Even though they are right next to the ocean, they do not splash each other with water. By the end of the season, their relationship ends in disaster. Who knows how strong their love could have grown if they had only seized the moment and splashed each other with water before it was too late.

*You can also fall in love by playing recreational sports with your prospective lover.*

51

**THE MONTAGE GLOSSARY**

# THE Hey I'm a Lifeguard, That's Right, a Lifeguard MONTAGE

By far the most popular type of *Baywatch* Montage, it is used to remind the viewer that this is in fact a show about lifeguards and those guys and girls in the red swimsuits are, you guessed it, lifeguards. But more than that, they serve to demonstrate just what a lifeguard does all day. Take '*Baywatch* Angels,' for instance. In the opening montage, C.J., Stephanie and Caroline show us that lifeguards run up and down the beach in slow motion and apply an awful lot of suntan lotion. And then in the dramatic conclusion to 'The Life You Save,' Mitch and company strut their lifesaving stuff by jumping from boats, saving drowning children, running in slow motion, riding wave-runners and generally just looking cool in sunglasses.

But you don't become a lifeguard overnight. It involves a lot of rigorous training and preparation. In 'Short Sighted,' Caroline and Logan practice their lifeguarding skills in a heart-pumping montage filled with slow-motion running, swimming and sit-ups. And in the opening montage of 'Trapped Beneath the Sea,' the new lifeguards save drowning swimmers and pose in cool sunglasses, as if to say, 'Hello. You may not recognize us, but we're *lifeguards*.'

'Hello. You may not recognize us, but we're lifeguards.'

# THE MONTAGE GLOSSARY

*That's right, I'm a lifeguard*

What about lifeguards who are returning to the show after an extended hiatus? We need to be reminded that they can still perform as a lifeguard. In 'Blindside,' returning lifeguard John D. Cort proves that he still has the stuff in a montage of running, standing, looking at pretty girls and pouring buckets of water on his face. After almost two-and-a-half minutes of this, we're convinced: 'Hey, this guy *is* a lifeguard.' In 'Fire With Fire,' we meet a new lifeguard on the beach named Andy. We can't help but wonder: 'Is he really a lifeguard?' After a lengthy montage in which he saves a drowning man, walks hand in hand with a child and mingles with a beautiful woman, the answer is a confident 'yes.'

There are many variations on the lifeguard montage. There is: 'Hey, I Used To Be a Lifeguard,' such as the kind used in 'The Red Knights.' In a series of black-and-white flashbacks, we watch lifeguards from the '20s in action, and discover that even back then, running in slow motion and wearing cool sunglasses were staples of California lifeguarding. But they had innovations that have since been abandoned, like carrying hot chicks on surfboards and standing on the beach in single file lines.

And this is just the beginning. There are countless examples of the lifeguard montage used to explain an occupation, including such notables as: 'Hey, I'm a High School Student' (Showdown at Malibu Beach High) and 'Hey, I'm a Biker' (Race Against Time).

*Do not leap to conclusions. This is, in fact, a lifeguard.*

### THE MONTAGE GLOSSARY

# THE *Flashback* MONTAGE

The flashback is one of the most innovative and creative montages of the *Baywatch oeuvre*. Most TV shows utilize the flashback, but too often it consists of little more than a brief overview of past events or boring, tiresome dialogue. But *Baywatch* knows that a flashback can be fun! Their Flashback Montages are accompanied by toe-tapping pop songs, and often involve big-breasted women even when it's not appropriate.

There are many reasons for using the Flashback Montage, but most often it's because something horrible and life-threatening is happening to a character. In 'Freefall,' Mitch has two full-length flashbacks of his *Baywatch* career, both of which use songs taken from David Hasselhoff's first solo album. The first flashback occurs when he thinks he's going to die, and the next flashback arrives when he thinks he's dead. The naysayers may say that one flashback was enough, but with a career as exciting and montage-worthy as Mitch Buchannon's, two flashbacks are hardly enough!

In 'Vacation: Part Two,' Stephanie is slowly dying on a deserted island and she has a disturbing flashback of her youth. In it, the adolescent Stephanie plays in the leaves with a group of multi-racial children. Eventually she gets on a swing, swings too high and falls into the ocean. We follow her into the water only to discover that she has grown into a woman. Her mother calls to her from a distance, but when she awakens she discovers that it is actually Mitch. Does this mean that

*Are these breasts appropriate?*

## THE MONTAGE GLOSSARY

### LET'S GET THIS STRAIGHT ...

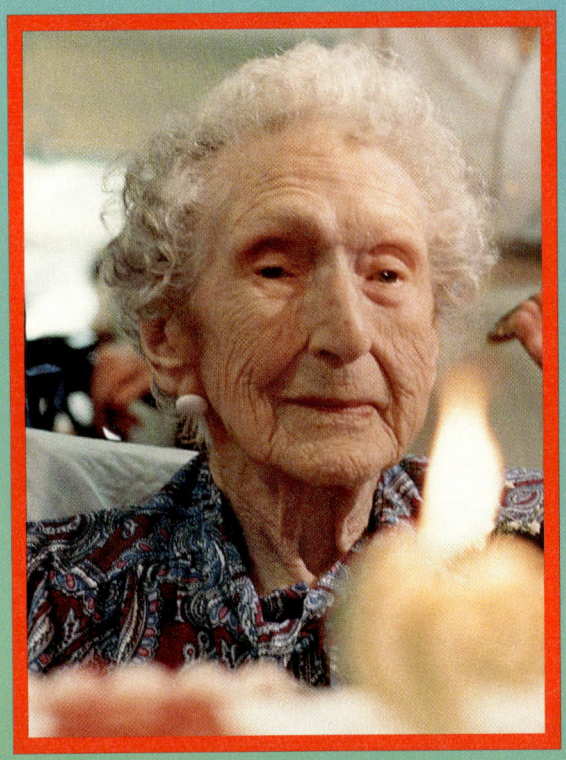

**Stephanie's Mum**

*Mitch Buchannon*

Stephanie thinks of Mitch as her mother? The montage never makes this clear, but we are left with a disturbing sensation that we've seen just a little *too much*.

Another reason that characters use Flashback Montages is when they are remembering a lost love or someone special to them from their past. In 'Tequila Bay,' Mitch remembers when he and Stephanie were in love, and they used to hang out at the gazebo, run and splash in the water, and then take a shower. In 'Shattered: Part Two,' Hobie remembers Mitch when he used to play football, fly kites and pick him up by the feet and spin him around in circles.

In 'Sky Rider,' Summer is told that Jimmy Slade is returning to *Baywatch*. We fade to a flashback montage of Jimmy Slade surfing, as if Summer was thinking, 'Hey, wasn't he that surfer guy?' That's probably all she needed to say, but as *Baywatch* knows, a picture is worth a thousand words, or at very least one.

But by far the most poignant montages are those depicting a horrifying memory in a character's life. In 'Lost & Found,' an old hippie remembers the '60s, in a montage which consists mostly of old news footage of protests, Martin Luther King and, of course, the Vietnam War. He is so upset by these memories that he sets fire to all of his old belongings. And in 'The Curator,' from *Baywatch Nights*, Caroline is haunted by a nightmarish Flashback Montage of psychos chasing her, being locked in a cage and a box full of kittens.

### THE MONTAGE GLOSSARY

# THE I'm Troubled MONTAGE

Not every character on *Baywatch* can enjoy the escapism of the Fantasy Montage. Many times, they must be content with their miserable lot, as they know there is no hope of their lives getting any better. But this doesn't mean they can't have their own montage. Just feeling bad is sometimes reason enough to enter montage territory.

Take 'Short Sighted,' for instance, one of the most classic examples of the Troubled Montage. In it, a sad midget walks on the beach and looks at all the tall people, while dragging a cooler that is easily twice his size. He doesn't want to be a midget, much less a midget on the beach, where he is stared at like a freak and attractive babes refuse to flirt with him. As he stews in his midget juices, the background music reassures him that being a midget is not as bad as he thinks. 'If they could see without their eyes,' the singer tells him, 'inside your soul you're ten feet tall.'

In 'Lost & Found,' a guy in a wheelchair sits next to the beach and feels bad that he can't walk. He watches all the kids have fun in the water and squishes his face into a pained expression that seems to say, 'Boy oh boy, I sure am crippled.' In 'Western Exposure,' a country singer sits in the park and feels bad because he misses his son. But instead of moping, he sings a song, a happy little ditty called 'Just My Way of Talking To God.' We can't help but hope he'll find his boy someday, if for no other reason than it'll get him to stop singing.

It isn't just guest characters who indulge in Troubled Montages. In a ground-breaking montage in 'Sky Rider,' Summer tries to decide whether she wants to date Matt or Slade. She thinks of Slade, surfing, and then Matt, running. Does she want Slade, the surfer, or Matt, the runner? The surfer or the runner? The runner or the surfer? So many choices. Let's think about it some more. There's Slade surfing. There's Matt running. Hmmm.

*Being a midget is not as bad as you think.*

## THE MONTAGE GLOSSARY

*Making a pig of yourself with food is guaranteed to scare unwanted women away.*

# THE Date MONTAGE

While most montages expand upon a simple theme, a Date Montage takes a big event and condenses it into just under two minutes. After all, we don't need to see everything that happened on a date, just the highlights. And if possible, we'd like to skip the dialogue too and just listen to a catchy pop tune.

The most common type of Date Montage is the bad date. In 'Red Wind,' Mitch takes a married woman on a date designed to scare her away so she'll go back to her geekish husband. Mitch makes a pig of himself with food, takes her on vomit-inducing carnival rides, drops ice cream on her dress, and flirts openly with attractive women. Although used primarily to summarize the date, this particular montage also allows Mitch to display his wide repertoire of funny faces and bug-eyed double-takes. In 'Freefall,' C.J. and her current beau are chased by paparazzi, à la The Beatles' 'Hard Days Night.' In it, C.J. shows us that she too can make funny faces with the best of them.

Then there is the romantic date, which differs from the bad date only by the absence of funny faces. In 'Point Doom,' Matt plays pool with a sexy biker. She walks around the table, looking sexy and preparing to shoot. Matt is impressed. She shakes her hips and puts a lot of chalk on her stick. Strangely, they never get around to actually playing pool, but perhaps that's the point. In 'Princess of Tides,' Mitch and a mysterious woman have a date, which involves mostly riding the merri-go-round and eating cotton candy.

But not all dates are of a sexual nature. Sometimes even friends go on dates. In 'Blindside,' Hobie and his new giant buddy go to a carnival and win big prizes. The giant demonstrates his skill at the bean bag toss, and he is rewarded with many stuffed animals. But it's not all fun and games. The giant is so excited by winning that he gets a crazy Manson-like look in his eyes. When he and Hobie walk off together in the montage's closer, we are left with an eerie sensation that something horrible is going to happen to Hobie later.

*Is something horrible going to happen to Hobie later?*

57

## THE MONTAGE GLOSSARY

# THE Fantasy MONTAGE

Believe it or not, the characters on *Baywatch* are not always happy with their life in sunny California. They often fantasize about a world that is better than *Baywatch*, if such a thing is possible. The Fantasy Montage allows us a rare glimpse into the dreams of these unhappy souls, and shows us that even on the beach, there's room for improvement.

Many of these Fantasy Montages involve potential romances, the one true desire of any Baywatcher. In 'Masquerade,' Mitch fantasizes that Stephanie is a sexy lounge singer and he has facial hair. Apparently this is supposed to be some kind of homage to *Gone With the Wind*, but as far as we can remember, Scarlett

*'A D cup ... just what I always wanted.'*

O'Hara never sang in a bar or writhed erotically on a piano. But this fantasy is in black-and-white which, as any romance fan knows, means 'Classic Old Movie.'

In 'Stakeout at Surfrider Beach,' Mitch fantasizes about walking with a beautiful Italian actress on the beach. They are eventually joined by Hobie, and then a bevy of young children. Mitch seems to be

*'Do I look like I'd writhe erotically on a piano?'*

## THE MONTAGE GLOSSARY

expressing a desire to start a family, and perhaps even to sire his children on the beach. In 'Strangers Among Us,' Summer fantasizes about a romantic encounter with Slade in what appears to be a tropical jungle sauna. They swim in the water together, then sit on the cement-beach to dry off and stare seductively at each other. They never actually kiss, but after swimming a few laps with the woman you love, who needs kissing?

In 'K-Gas: The Groove Yard of Solid Gold,' a wacky overweight DJ fantasizes about being a lifeguard and running on the beach towards C.J. They meet and dance around in circles. Of course, we know that his dreams can never become a reality, because he is fat.

Even Fantasy Montages that are not initially about romance find a way to bring it back to love. In both 'Second Time Around' and 'Livin' On Fault Line: Part One,' Hobie fantasizes about being a rock star, which mostly involve him being chased by prepubescent girls. Why exactly Hobie wants to get away from a pack of horny girls is never fully explained. Considering that he has never had a girlfriend that lasted more than a few episodes, we're a little concerned.

*His dreams can never become a reality because he is fat.*

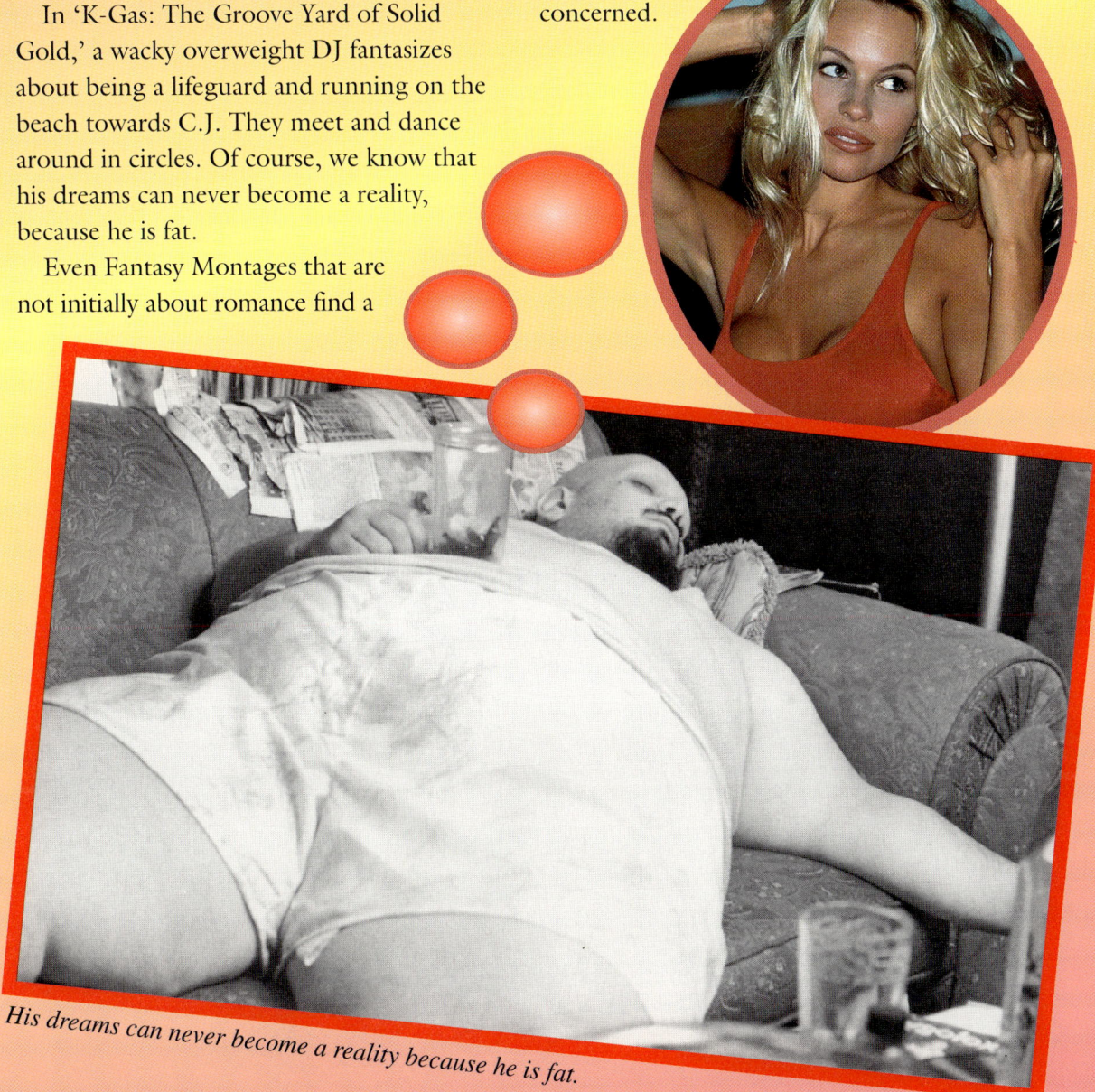

# Introducing Your Child To
# BAYWATCH

Children are our future, and so it is our responsibility to prepare them for the world of tomorrow. Your children's survival on Planet *Baywatch* depends on their ability to assimilate into the culture of lifeguards and California beaches. That's why it is of utmost importance that you begin their training at an early age, allowing them the opportunity to develop into strong, healthy, educated *Baywatch* citizens. It could mean the difference between your offspring finding happiness and success in life, or ending up alone, bitter and excluded from society. The choice is up to you.

If you are an expectant parent, or have a son or daughter who is still in their formative years, it is not too late for you to begin educating them in the values and aesthetics of *Baywatch*. To aid you in this process, we have provided you with a brief primer course that you can use on your own child. Remember, teach the children today, and they will grow up to be happy and prosperous lifeguards tomorrow.

*A child who watches Baywatch will never succumb to the pressures of drug abuse.*

60

*Episodes of* Baywatch *should constantly be playing when the child is awake, and kept at a loud volume so that it is impossible to ignore.*

## 1. Your Child's First Day

It is never too soon to introduce your child to the warm, comforting concepts of *Baywatch*. In fact, we would suggest surrounding them with *Baywatch* imagery as soon as they enter your home. Prepare for your child's arrival by decorating the room he or she will occupy to resemble a California beach. Cover the floors with sand and paint the walls in a bright blue color. Both the mother and father should wear only official *Baywatch* uniforms (orange swim trunks for the guys, orange one-piece swimsuits for the gals) and provide the child with the same. Episodes of *Baywatch* should constantly be playing when the child is awake, and kept at a loud volume so that it is impossible to ignore. If it becomes too much for the child to take, substitute the TV show with selections from the *Baywatch* soundtrack, which will provide some relief while continuing to re-reinforce the presence of *Baywatch* in his life.

## 2. Early Training

Your child must become familiar early on with the importance of lifeguards and his dependence on them for survival. When bathing your child, introduce him to the rescue can, which should always be stored near the tub. When he has become aware of the rescue can and comfortable with using it, it is time to demonstrate its purpose. Push your child under the water, filling his lungs with water and providing him with the sensation of drowning. Then give him the rescue can and allow him to return to the surface. After a few of these traumatizing experiences, your child will begin to understand that the rescue can is a good thing and brings relief and life.

It is particularly important that your child becomes comfortable with the water. If possible, buy a pool for your toddler. If you don't have the income for this, make sure that your child spends as much time as possible in

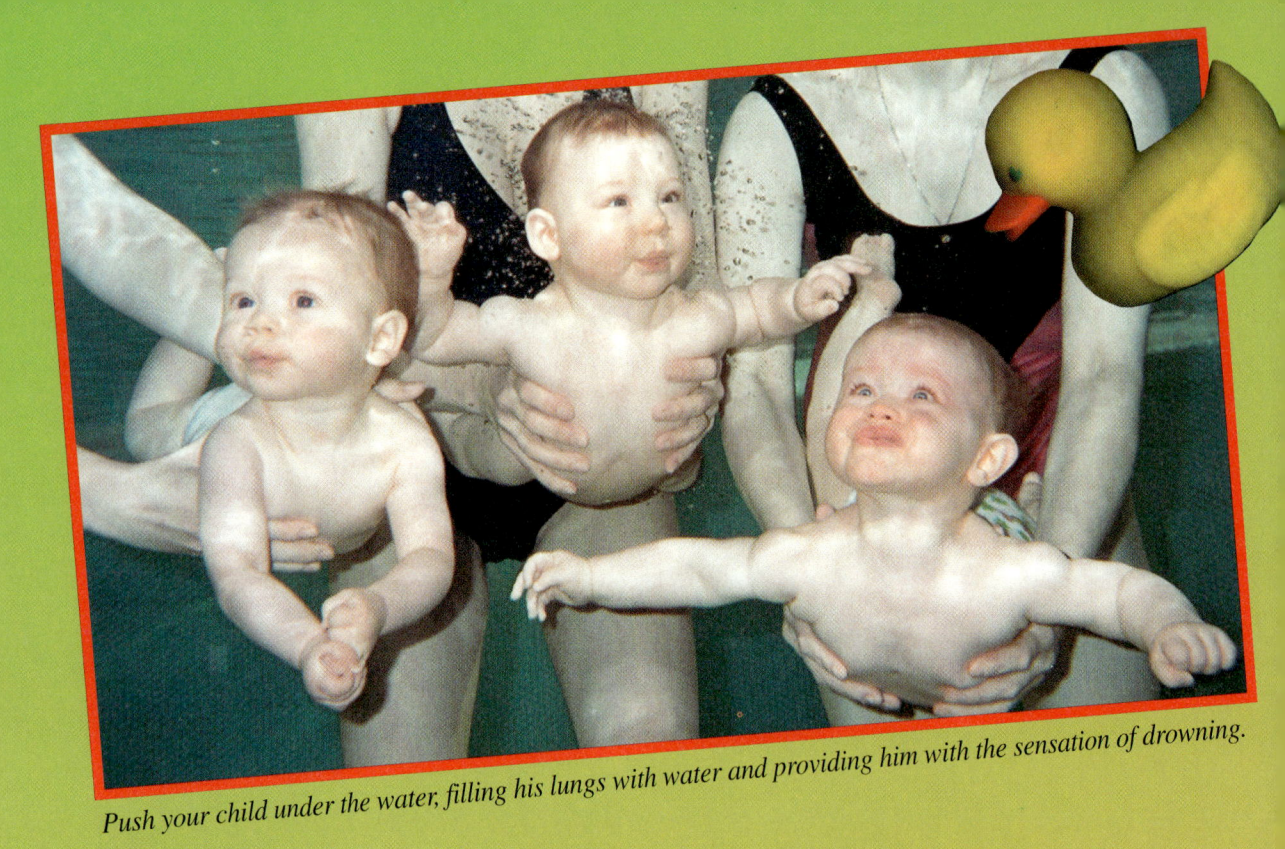

*Push your child under the water, filling his lungs with water and providing him with the sensation of drowning.*

the bathtub. The bathtub should be used for naps, meals and playtime, and he should only be allowed to leave it if his skin has begun to wrinkle to the point of painful irritation.

At six months, it is time to begin working on your child's tan. Have him sit out in the sun for a minimum of four hours a day. (Be sure to use an adequate suntan lotion, as a baby's skin tends to burn easily.) During the winter months, supply him with a tanning machine to ensure a consistent and golden-brown skin tone throughout the year. At the same time, start him on a strict and vigorous workout regime, with weight-lifting, jogging and aerobic exercises.

## 3. The Importance of Watching BAYWATCH

As we said before, your child should be constantly exposed to *Baywatch* episodes. But there may come a time when your child tries to resist this stimulus. If you notice that your child is attempting to turn off the TV, or has succeeded in doing so, you may need to provide him with some compelling reasons for continuing to watch. When *Baywatch* is not playing, give him some frightening examples of what life would be like without the show. Speak to him in a loud, harsh voice, spank him for no reason, sporadically burst into fits of rage or tears, serve him bland, tasteless food and kill his pets. When *Baywatch* has been turned back on, shower him with love and affection, making him feel comfortable and secure. This is a form of 'behavioralism,' as pioneered by B.F. Skinner, which will convince the child that *Baywatch* brings pleasure and the absence of *Baywatch* brings pain. This will guarantee that your child becomes a lifelong *Baywatch* fan and will never develop a free-thinking personality that will interfere with his ability to function as a responsible citizen of Planet *Baywatch*.

## 4. Playtime

All children have active imaginations, and this should be encouraged ... to a point. Let your child know that he is welcome to enjoy a fantasy life, so long as it involves the characters and plot possibilities of *Baywatch*. You may want to buy your child a *Baywatch Barbie®* (available now in toy stores everywhere), but be aware that these dolls don't resemble any specific character and therefore may confuse your child. Better yet, use these specifically designed cut-outs to create your own *Baywatch* play-toys. Simply glue the cut-outs to a stick of wood and you're done. They won't need another toy for the remainder of their childhood.

## 5. Friendships

Inevitably, your child will want to make contact with the outside world, and that's fine. But make sure he knows that there are only two types of people in the world: lifeguards and people who hate lifeguards. Warn him to stay away from boys and girls who are not fans of *Baywatch*, as they are tools of the devil and want nothing more than to take away his rescue can and drown him.

As your child reaches adulthood, he will learn that his strict *Baywatch* upbringing was essential to his development, and he will be thankful that he had parents who cared enough about him to invest in his future. And then one day, when a man in dark sunglasses and a trench coat comes to his door and says, 'I'll be there,' your son or daughter will be able to say, in a voice full of confidence and understanding, 'Never you fear, no no don't you fear.'

# Everything I Ever Really Needed To Know About Life I Learned From Being Trapped In Underwater Caverns

If you live in Southern California, the odds are good that you're going to be trapped underwater sooner or later. Most of the time people end up in underwater caverns, but you can also be trapped inside a sinking offshore oil rig, an armored truck or even under an avalanche of rocks. Whatever the reason, it seems like an awful lot of the characters on *Baywatch* end up stuck underwater. Why does this happen so much? *Baywatch* knows that sometimes the most important lessons in life can only be learned in the midst of a suffocating encounter.

### Underwater Ordeal
C.J. and Stephanie are trapped in an underwater cavern after an avalanche cuts off the exit.

### Lesson Learned
You shouldn't trust every man you meet.

### Underwater Ordeal
Two female Junior Lifeguards go exploring and fall into an underwater cavern.

### Lesson Learned
Teamwork is important.

### Underwater Ordeal
Summer, Matt and Slade venture into an underwater cavern in search of a missing surfboard and are attacked by an octopus.

### Lesson Learned
A healthy diet is the best way to maintain good self-esteem.

64

## Underwater Ordeal
A plane crashes in the ocean, trapping Hobie and Gayle 40 feet underwater.

## Lesson Learned
A son deserves to live with his father.

## Underwater Ordeal
Eddie and Shauni are trapped inside an armored truck that falls into the water and sinks.

## Lesson Learned
Commitment is necessary for a successful relationship.

## Underwater Ordeal
The leader of a geological survey team is planting a seismometer in the Malibu fault when an earthquake hits, causing an underwater avalanche that traps him under a rock formation.

## Lesson Learned
California sucks.

'Does California suck, or what?'

# Hairwatch

## GREAT HAIR MOMENTS ON BAYWATCH

Many critics have accused *Baywatch* of concentrating too heavily on exposed flesh and bulging swimsuits. But more studied scholars of the show know that *Baywatch* gives equal time to other important aspects of California life, such as hair. Interesting hair is not just a staple on the show, it also directly affects character development, thematic content and the fate of *Baywatch*'s actors and actresses. Here are a few examples of some of the more memorable moments in *Baywatch* hair.

## Stephanie Cuts Off Her Hair

When Lieutenant Stephanie Holden cut off her brunette locks two seasons ago, it marked a new beginning both for her character and for womankind. Not only did it free her from the stereotypes of the big-haired *Baywatch* babe, it also signaled an end to her on-again, off-again flirtation with Mitch. The cutting of her locks represented a cutting of the ties between her and Mitch, and allowed her to engage in another on-again, off-again flirtation with a world-traveling oceanographer. It could also be argued that her short hair was in some way responsible for her developing skin cancer. Granted, we can't really prove this, but it's just a gut feeling.

*Cancer-free.*

*Uh-oh!*

# Summer Goes Brunette

Summer Quinn was one of the more popular characters on the show, thanks in part to her fetching, golden blonde hair. Deciding to change her hair color to brunette for the fourth season was a risky choice, especially considering that there was already one other brunette on the show. But the producers allowed the blonde rape to take place and it ultimately destroyed both the character and the actress. Summer Quinn was taken off the show that very season, and Nicole Eggert, the actress who played Summer, went on to star in a series of miserable made-for-TV movies.

*No fun today, no job tomorrow.*

# Mustache for Mitch

In 'Masquerade,' Mitch and Stephanie disguise themselves as rich honeymooners in an attempt to lure some pirates into a trap. Although Stephanie goes whole-hog, putting on a blonde wig and heavy make-up, the only costume that Mitch chooses is a fake mustache. And much to everybody's surprise, it works! Nobody recognizes him, and the pirates show up as planned. But the sight of Mitch with facial hair causes Stephanie to experience such lust that she ends up almost sleeping with him. The message is clear: facial hair acts as an aphrodisiac. It may result in unintentional fornication.

*Who is this guy?*

*Facial hair may result in unintentional fornication.*

# TOOLS of the TRADE

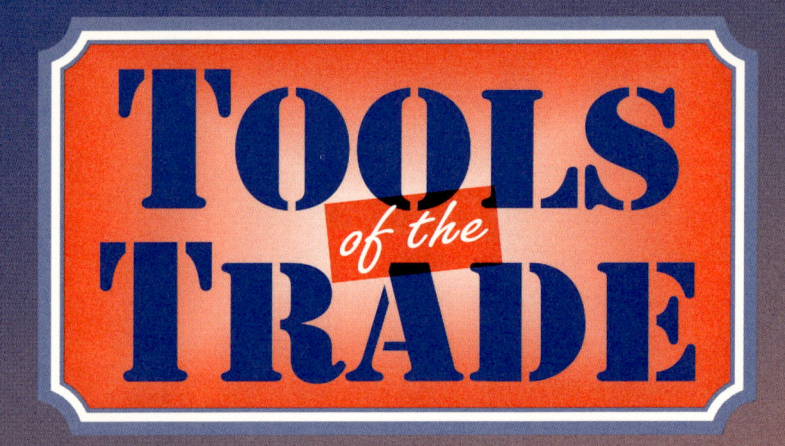

### (Is That a Life Preserver or Are You Just Glad to See Me?)

One of the main tools used by the lifeguards of *Baywatch* is the red 'rescue can.' This bright red, rigid float is attached to a rope and allows guards to rescue victims without having to make physical contact. But in the danger-ridden world of *Baywatch*, these rescue cans have a multitude of other uses besides saving lives. For instance …

• Protecting yourself from crowbars swung by evil convict wives ('Tentacles: Part One')

• Tripping serial killers who are trying to sneak into the *Baywatch* office ('The Tower')

*'Are you staring at my can?'*

- Helps viewers tell the difference between drowning lifeguards and drowning civilians ('Someone to *Baywatch* Over Me')

- Makes dweebish husbands look cool and win back the affection of their adulterous wives ('Red Wind')

- A place to attach breather masks to avoid giving mouth-to-mouth to icky AIDS patients ('A Little Help From My Friend')

- Beating up visiting friends from Philadelphia ('Second Wave')

- Spinning on finger to wow the babes (opening credits to every episode)

Fame at last!

# BAYWATCH CARES ABOUT THE ISSUES

*Baywatch* is more than just sun and fun. It tackles the big issues of our times and offers fresh, even startling insights. Unlike most TV dramas, or for that matter most political movements or major religions, *Baywatch* wants to make this world a better place for you and me.

*Baywatch says:* 'Hey kids! Don't fool around with Satan! He's got an eating disorder!'

## MAJOR ISSUE
### Exploitative Oil Companies

**How Baywatch Is Making A Difference**
C.J. asks Matt to wear a 'No Drilling' T-shirt at a beach volleyball tournament.

## MAJOR ISSUE
### Cancer

**How Baywatch Is Making A Difference**
Mitch proposes to a woman with cancer, then takes her to the beach to die.

## MAJOR ISSUE
### Bulimia

**How Baywatch Is Making A Difference**
Summer decides to seek professional help for her eating disorder after barely escaping from an octopus attack.

*Did an octopus force Diana to seek help?*

## MAJOR ISSUE
### Underage drinking

**How Baywatch Is Making A Difference**
A daredevil motorcycle stuntman who encourages underage drinking is kicked off the beach and taunted by sober children.

## MAJOR ISSUE
### Pollution

**How Baywatch Is Making A Difference**
Surfers are getting strange skin rashes from water pollution, so the Beach Boys show up and perform on the beach.

## MAJOR ISSUE
### Sexual Harassment

**How Baywatch Is Making A Difference**
Neely accuses Matt of sexual harassment. Even though he is innocent, Neely refuses to drop the charges. Then she gets kidnapped by pirates.

## MAJOR ISSUE
### Blindness

**How Baywatch Is Making A Difference**
John D. Cort discovers that he's going blind, so Mitch agrees to help him smuggle ancient artifacts across the Mexican border.

*Cool kids crash Matt's party and do drugs.*

## MAJOR ISSUE
### Drugs

**How Baywatch Is Making A Difference**
Some 'cool' kids crash Matt's party and do drugs, then almost drown in the pool. When Mitch finds out about the incident, he calls it 'pretty stupid.'

## MAJOR ISSUE
### Leukemia

**How Baywatch Is Making A Difference**
A young boy with leukemia needs a bone marrow transplant, but his donor is missing. Mitch discovers that he has been kidnapped by cocaine smugglers and returns the donor in the nick of time.

## MAJOR ISSUE
### Alzheimer's Disease

**How Baywatch Is Making A Difference**
Mitch suspects that his mother has Alzheimer's when she leaves her carry-on baggage on the plane.

## MAJOR ISSUE
### Skin Cancer

**How Baywatch Is Making A Difference**
Stephanie discovers that she has skin cancer, so she wanders around the beach and screams at swimmers about their suntan lotion.

*Oil up, you guys*

## MAJOR ISSUE
### Gigantism

**How Baywatch Is Making A Difference**
A gentle giant meets Hobie and decides that he'd rather sell hand-carved figurines on the beach than star in a freak show.

## MAJOR ISSUE
### Dwarfism

**How Baywatch Is Making A Difference**
Midgets show up frequently on the show, and only once are characterized as goofy little 'Santa's Helpers.'

*With my implants I'm a 22A*

73

## THE MOST REVEALING PHOTO EVER!!

# C.J. IS ELECTRIFYING SEXPOT

A truly shocking videotape was delivered to our offices by a man claiming to be an ex-employee of All-American Productions, David Hasselhoff's production company. The tape portrays, as shown, a figure who looks remarkably like C.J. Parker being disassembled and/or repaired by a group of technicians. A panel of experts were called in to examine photos of the world's sultriest cyberbabe. Their analysis as noted, shows in explicit detail what makes C.J., or the PARKERBOT, tick. So is it possible? Will a shocked world be able to cope? Is C.J. Parker really a cyborg?

The ex-employee, who prefers to remain anonymous, claims that at any given moment as many as three Parkerbots are active. "There's the one they use for exterior shots, one for interior work, and they fire up the third one if she's required at a press conference."

Further, because of the extremely physical nature of BAYWATCH and the frequent immersions that each Parkerbot must endure, AAP manufactures two new Parkerbots every year, according to our source. But they are far from identical.

"The producers keep making changes and adjustments. They're never happy," he testified. "If you watch the show, you'll notice her breasts keep getting larger, her lips fuller. If they don't stop this sometime soon, it's going to get completely out of hand. People will begin to notice."

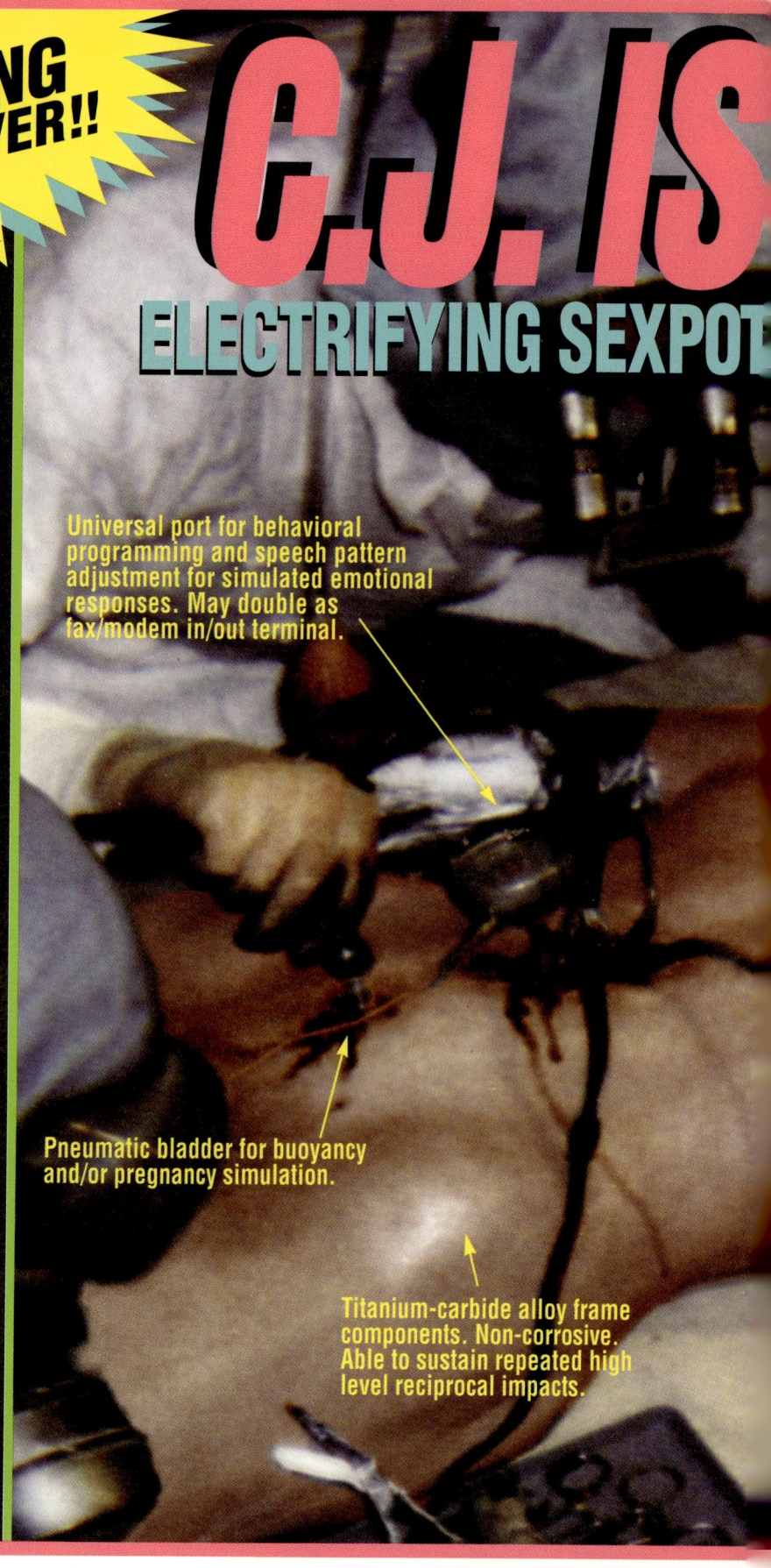

**Universal port for behavioral programming and speech pattern adjustment for simulated emotional responses. May double as fax/modem in/out terminal.**

**Pneumatic bladder for buoyancy and/or pregnancy simulation.**

**Titanium-carbide alloy frame components. Non-corrosive. Able to sustain repeated high level reciprocal impacts.**

# A CYBORG?!
## GETS HER BANG FROM *BATTERIES!!*

**TIM FIMIA**
*Corres.-Chicago*

**Motion actuation adjustment. allows real time slow-motion movement. Encloses infrared global positioning software.**

**Feature set restarts on "pout".**

**Oral fueling unit. Fuel substance believed to be a thick petroleum-ammonia paste.**

**Micro-servo drives control programmed facial expression.**

**Expandable batteries with 220 volt a/c manual jacks.**

**Lower arm substructural damage, possibly sustained in stunt scene during recent episode involving sea-alligator.**

### ...AND SHE'S NO AIRHEAD!!

**This illicit photo shows an interior view of the Parkerbot cranium, with skull cap removed. An array of tools, lubricating oils and cosmetics assure that the Parkerbot is always "ready for servicing."**

## EXCLUSIVE
## *An Interview with*
# C.J. PARKER

By now everybody has interviewed Pamela Anderson Lee, but what we really wanted was a probing discussion with C.J. Parker. Most journalists would have shied away from such an impossible task, but we found a way to make it happen. Using quotes taken from her character's dialogue on *Baywatch*, we were able to conduct the first-ever interview with a fictional character.

And now, C.J. Parker ... in her own words.

**Planet *Baywatch*: Did you always want to be a lifeguard?**
C.J. Parker: I can't imagine doing anything else. My mom said I was born with a red rescue can in my hands.

**P.B.: What qualifies you to be a lifeguard?**
C.J.: I've seen every episode of *Love Boat*.

**P.B.: You've had your share of heated romances on *Baywatch*. What was your most memorable?**
C.J.: I really loved Craig the Marine Biologist. It was one of those fated meetings. There we were, both underwater, and something just clicked. It was so romantic.

**P.B.: You've had some failed romances as well. What happened with the Priest?**
C.J.: I didn't do anything to encourage Father Ryan! I did nothing to be ashamed of. It was a total misunderstanding.

'I didn't do anything to encourage Father Ryan! It was a total misunderstanding.'

**P.B.: Is there any tried and true way of mending a broken heart?**
C.J.: If I figure that one out, I'm gonna write a best-seller. The hurt still hurts.

**P.B.: What advice would you give to men who want to seduce you?**
C.J.: Don't give me a passionate kiss unless you have the time or the inclination to carry it through.

**P.B.: Don't you have an interest in New Age Philosophy?**
C.J.: I think anything is possible. I like to meditate and chant and ring chimes. It's sexy.

**P.B.: What's the latest New Age trend?**
C.J.: If enough people think peace, it can happen.

**P.B.: I don't follow you. Could you elaborate a little?**
C.J.: There's a whole series of cosmic convergences happening. It's throwing up a lot of really unusual energy, but we need to harness that energy for the good of mankind.

**P.B.: Pardon me for saying this, but that sounds a little wacky.**
C.J.: If there can be aliens, why can't there be elves?

**P.B.: What the hell is that supposed to mean?**
C.J.: Your system is polluted. You should at least chant with me.

**P.B.: You have no idea what you're talking about, do you?**
C.J.: You're not the kind of person I need to waste my energy on. The universe will make sure you get what you deserve.

*'Don't give me a passionate kiss unless you have the time or inclination to carry it through.'*

*'If there can be aliens, why can't there be elves?'*

*'You're not the kind of person I need to waste my energy on. The universe will make sure you get what you deserve.'*

# THE BEAUTY BECOMES A BEAST!!

Possibly the actual female upon which the Parkerbot was modeled. Cute.

According to our source, each version of Parkerbots is numbered, with the original models being the Parkerbot Mark One. The model currently in use is supposedly an example of the Parkerbot Mark Six.

Planet Baywatch was able to obtain this microfilm copy of a concept rendering for the Parkerbot MARK SEVEN, the next generation. "They've completely abandoned the pretense that she's human," our source whispers, "It's quite grotesque."

One of three current Parkerbots in use, the Mark Six. Harder, angular. A bit unsettling.

A.A.P. CLASSIFIED A.A.P.

FOR YOUR EYES ONLY

Mark Seven-1

Artists conception of Parkerbot, ULTRA series, Mark seven. A horrifying example of unchecked Scientific ambition. Sickening.

78

# History Repeats Itself

## Mitch Buchannon and Oscar Wilde

Oscar Wilde is probably best known for his sardonic wit, homosexual antics and writing such classic plays as *A Woman of No Importance*, *An Ideal Husband*, and *The Importance of Being Earnest*. As far as we know, he never spent time on the beaches of California or had any ambitions to become a lifeguard. One would think that he and Mitch Buchannon had absolutely nothing in common, but we suspect otherwise. Below are quotes taken from the writings of Oscar Wilde mixed in with quotes from Mitch. Can you tell which is which?

> The only way to get rid of a temptation is to yield to it

1. 'The only way to get rid of a temptation is to yield to it.'
2. 'Romance is in short supply these days. Men just don't go around ripping women's clothes off anymore. You have to *ask*.'
3. 'As long as a woman can look ten years younger than her own daughter, she is perfectly satisfied.'
4. 'Besides her looks, her talent and her intelligence, she really didn't have much to offer.'
5. 'I don't want money. It is people who pay their bills who want that, and I never pay mine.'
6. 'We spent our honeymoon in Hawaii. Every time there's a volcanic eruption, I think of her.'
7. 'One should never do anything that one cannot talk about after dinner.'
8. 'The male ego is a disease. In my case, possibly terminal.'

(Answers: 2, 4, 6 and 8 are Mitch Buchannon; 1, 3, 5 and 7 are Oscar Wilde)

> Every time there's a volcanic eruption, I think of her

# THE Love PAGE

In 'Home Is Where the Heart Is,' Matt Brody returns to *Baywatch* after a short hiatus and asks Mitch what's happened since he's been gone. Mitch takes a deep breath and tells him: 'Caroline says C.J. is interested in Cody as a way of getting over you, but Stephanie is Cody's swim coach and I see a May/September thing developing there, now Caroline and Cody are close friends, *very* close friends, which makes Logan very jealous because he's very interested in Caroline as long as it doesn't interfere with his hitting on other girls, especially Neely, who was seen kissing Cody at a Beach Boys concert.'

Well, what'd you expect him to say? 'We saved some swimmers from drowning'? C'mon, this is *Baywatch*. You can't expect a lifeguard to worry about saving lives until he's got a date for Saturday night. A guy's gotta have priorities, right? And any right-thinking lifeguard wouldn't dream of jumping into the ocean to pull out a sinking child unless she knows that some cute guy is waiting to towel her off afterwards. This is California, where love is king. Accept it and you will find happiness and splendor. Deny it and it will destroy you.

*'There goes my date for Saturday night.'*

# Men Are From Mars, Women Are From Tower 12
## Some Things That *Baywatch* Has Taught Us About Love

- Pointing a gun at a woman is not always the best way to make her like you.
- Sometimes, push-ups can be better than sex.

*Sometimes, push-ups can be better than sex.*

- In Australia, men seduce women by hiring thugs to push them into the ocean.
- If two people are frolicking in the water, splashing and pushing each other under the waves, they are probably in love.
- Any gift that a woman gives a man is probably stolen property.
- Chicks dig seals.
- Guys with long hair mistreat women. If you want your guy to treat you right, make him get a haircut.

*Guys with long hair mistreat women.*

- Biker chicks are nothing but trouble.
- Women with mysterious pasts are nothing but trouble.
- Ex-girlfriends are nothing but trouble.
- Women in general are nothing but trouble.
- The only sure-fire way to win the heart of a woman is to be an environmentalist.
- Since no one actually has sex, where babies come from (there have been two on the show) is not exactly clear.

*Biker chicks are nothing but trouble.*

*Children who fall in love usually end up dead.*

- Children who fall in love usually end up being beaten up by bigger kids, attacked by killer jellyfish, chased by gangster hitmen or dead.
- Bungee-jumping is not a good way to settle a lovers' tiff.
- Cheating on your girlfriend can, in rare cases, cause blindness.
- Marriages never work, and usually result in plane crashes, comas or the sudden appearance of World War II mines.

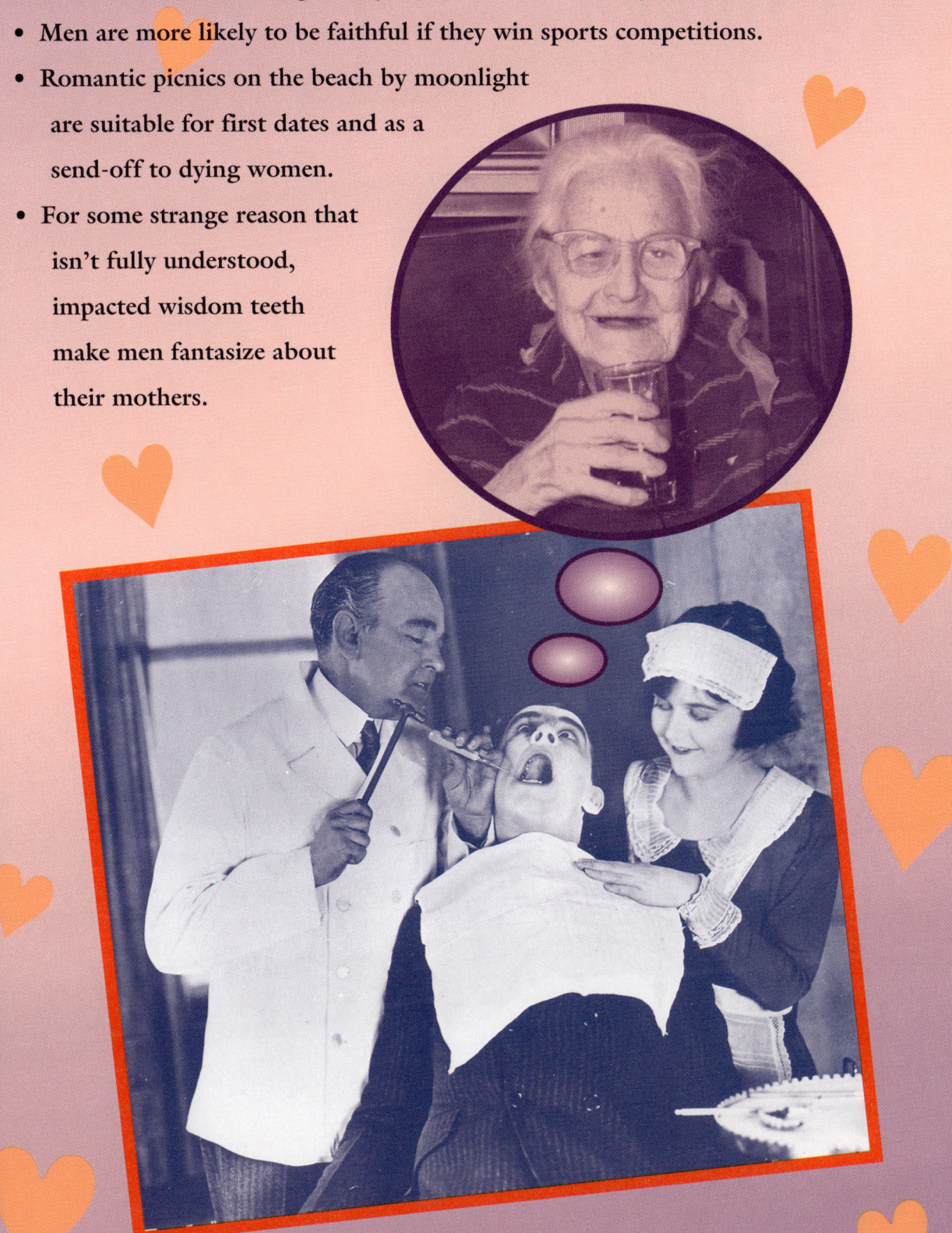

- True love lasts, on average, forty-two minutes (excluding commercial time).
- Men are more likely to be faithful if they win sports competitions.
- Romantic picnics on the beach by moonlight are suitable for first dates and as a send-off to dying women.
- For some strange reason that isn't fully understood, impacted wisdom teeth make men fantasize about their mothers.

# 'I Think I Love Him... Uh-oh, He's Got a Gun!'

***BAYWATCH* INSTRUCTS US WHEN TO FALL IN LOVE AND WHEN TO RUN AWAY**

So you say that love baffles you? You don't know when a romance is going well and when you should make a hasty retreat? Relax, *Baywatch* is here to help. Having gone through virtually hundreds of romances, these California lifeguards have devoted their lives to examining every fact of love. They know what makes love work, and what makes it go sour. Learn from their mistakes, and you might escape the heart-break that they've had to endure. That is, after all, their job.

**REASON TO FALL IN LOVE**
He's a sexy environmental investigator with a heart of gold and he wants to marry you.

**REASON TO FALL OUT OF LOVE**
He's in a decompression chamber.

84

**REASON TO FALL IN LOVE**
She's a strikingly attractive investigative reporter, and she thinks you're dreamy.

**REASON TO FALL OUT OF LOVE**
She's dead, and you're the prime suspect.

**REASON TO FALL IN LOVE**
You meet a handsome stranger at a San Diego hotel.

**REASON TO FALL OUT OF LOVE**
He's a ghost and wants to shove you off a tall building.

**REASON TO FALL IN LOVE**
He's a sexy guy who works with children.

**REASON TO FALL OUT OF LOVE**
He's a priest.

*Uh-oh, the sexy guy's a priest.*

I'M DROWNING! HELP

**REASON TO FALL IN LOVE**
A beautiful woman invites you to have dinner with her.

**REASON TO FALL OUT OF LOVE**
She has multiple personalities, and they both want to drown you in her basement.

**REASON TO FALL IN LOVE**
He gives you a necklace that he claims 'brings true love to whoever wears it.'

**REASON TO FALL OUT OF LOVE**
He dumps you and marries some old rich woman.

**REASON TO FALL IN LOVE**
He's a nice, attractive guy, even if he is holding you at gunpoint in your tower.

**REASON TO FALL OUT OF LOVE**
Your boss rescues you and throws him off the roof, shish-ke-bobbing him on a metal spike.

# The Greatest Love Stories of All Time

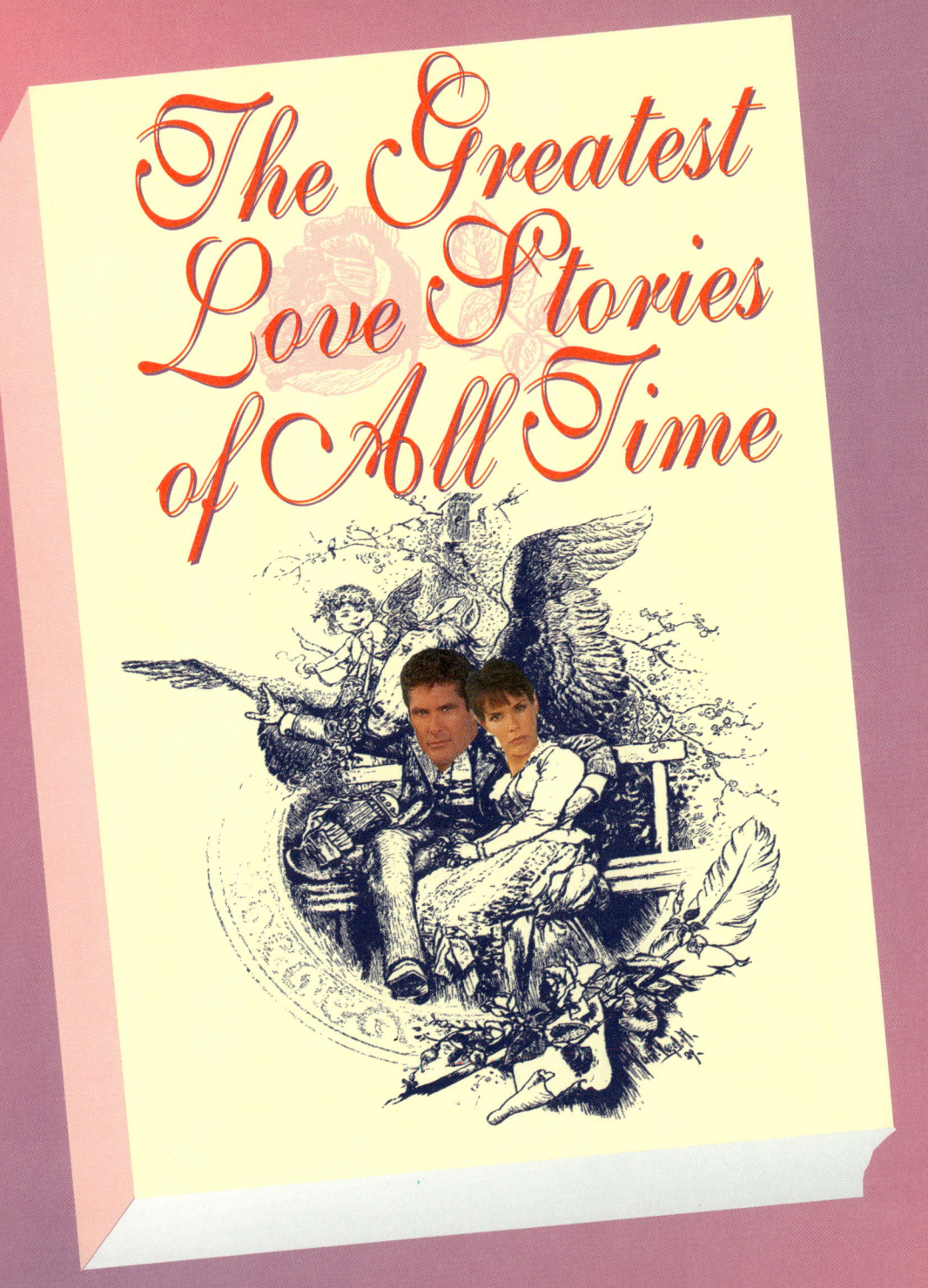

Boy meets girl, boy loses girl in freak accident, boy finds love in the arms of another boy who dresses just like Carmen Miranda. We already know this, and many other stories; the classics of all time, the books, plays, films and poems that make strong men swoon and short women giggle. *Baywatch* is about the now, yes, and in particular the now on the beach, but it is also about love – God's love, manly love, sisterly love, even doggie love. Energy may be equal to mass multiplied by the speed of light squared, but any *Baywatch* fan knows that love is the universal law. We'd say more, but we need to swoon right now.

## ROMEO AND JULIET

Romeo pines for Juliet, even though their parents disapprove. They eventually commit suicide, and their parents are remorseful.

Mitch pines for Tracy, even though his mother disapproves. Tracy dies of cancer, but his mother does not notice, as she has Alzheimer's Disease.

*Easy come, easy... er...*

*If we don't split up Hitler gets the yacht*

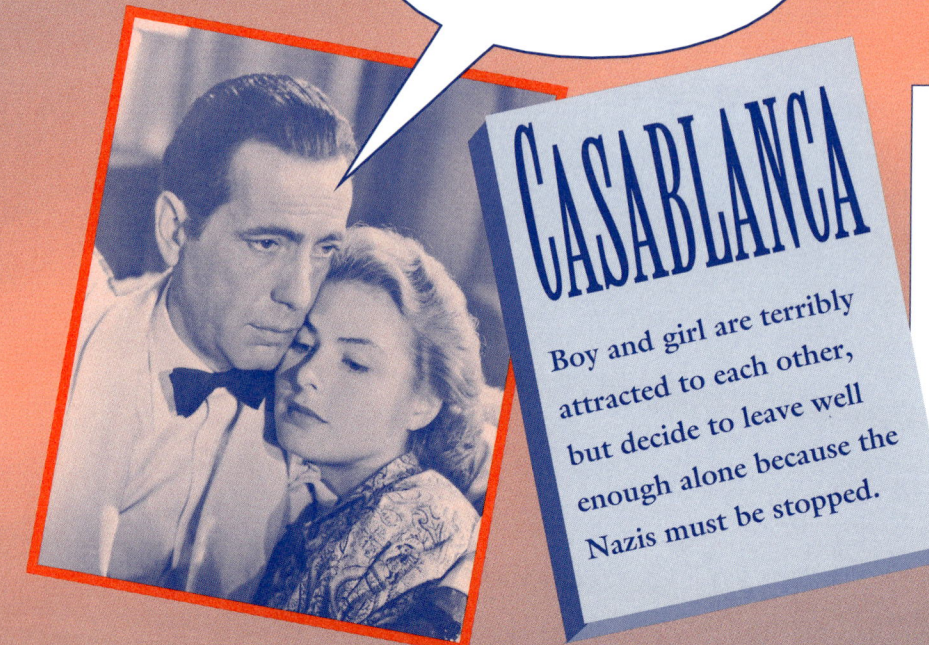

## CASABLANCA

Boy and girl are terribly attracted to each other, but decide to leave well enough alone because the Nazis must be stopped.

Mitch and Stephanie are terribly attracted to each other, but decide to leave well enough alone because of yacht thieves.

# Gone with the Wind

Boy and girl have long, on-again off-again relationship that ends when boy realizes girl is a manipulative bitch.

Mitch and Stephanie have a long, on-again off-again relationship that ends when Mitch realizes Stephanie is a manipulative bitch.

*Bitch to the rescue!*

# Wuthering Heights

Woman is torn between a boring lover and an abusive one, and eventually dies of heartbreak.

Summer is torn between the surfer and the lifeguard, and eventually decides to be alone because they bungee-jumped for her love.

# Deliverance

Burt Reynolds and a group of drinking buddies take a canoe trip, where they meet some rednecks who brutally rape one of them.

Mitch and a group of his lifeguard buddies take a whitewater rafting trip, where they meet C.J. Parker who, much to their disappointment, does not brutally rape any of them.

# HAZARDOUS TERRITORIES

Before you can become a successful *Baywatch* lifeguard, you need to be aware of the many hazardous territories that exist in the *Baywatch* universe, each of which possess a very specific threat to the visiting public. Know what to expect, and you will be better able to protect your swimmers.

- **The Pier:** Although it may seem harmless, the pier is filled with hazards, most notably visiting pirates and/or diamond smugglers who dock their boats there. Pedestrians who wander too close to the pier always fall into the water, and boats that sail too close will undoubtedly hit it and sink. Under the docks is where most of the action takes place, such as small boys being chased by gangsters or psychotic killers hiding from the police. Also be aware that scarabs laden with dynamite will always head straight for the pier.

- **The Boardwalk:** A favorite for high-speed chases, either by foot, car, skateboard or rollerblade. There is an unusual abundance of con artists and political assassins, most of whom like to assault or chase the children of lifeguards.

- **Lovers' Cove:** A popular romantic spot up the coast, its waters are filled with Man O' War jellyfish who attack lifeguards.

- **Tequila Bay:** The turf of 'Shooters,' a violent gang of surfer punks who put barbed wire in the water to keep unwanted surfers away.

*Political assassins often hang out on the boardwalk.*

*Nearly dead.*

- **Whitewater Cove:** A dangerous and rocky surfing site, it is used mostly for competitions among dueling lovers. Beware of the 'surfboard graveyard,' an underwater cavern that sucks in surfboards and has an octopus that attacks bulimic women.

- **Point Furman Bluffs:** A favorite site for hang-gliding, especially by drunk teenage punks who steal gliders from lifeguards and fall to their death.

- **Point Dumme Road:** Used mostly for motorcycle races, this road borders huge cliffs that are used by evil biker thugs and jealous lovers to knock Matt Brody to his repeated near death.

- **Surfrider Beach:** Pretty much like any other beach on *Baywatch*, except that visiting Italian actresses tend to get robbed here.

- **Bahama Mama's:** A haunt of the Red Knights, an old group of *Baywatch* lifeguards. Well known for its bar brawls, regular customers with nicknames like 'Corky' and allowing the mothers of lifeguards to sing in public.

- **Will Rogers Beach:** The favorite spot of visiting psychopaths, who like to kidnap lifeguards and hold them at gun-point in their towers.

*She may laugh but the killer octopus lurks in the surfboard graveyard.*

91

# Mitch Buchannon's Guide to *Successful Parenting*

*'You feel like crying? You feel like yelling? You feel like pizza?'*
*Mitch Buchannon*

Are you a single father raising a young boy in Venice, California? Even if you're not, you could stand to learn a thing or two from Mitch Buchannon. As the most successful father on *Baywatch*, where the majority of parents are either dead-beats, abusive or dead, Mitch has a monopoly on child-raising excellence, and if we want our own children to grow up to be as well adjusted as Hobie Buchannon, we should follow in the footsteps of Mitch.

**Problem with Son**
He refuses to do his chores.

**Mitch Solution**
Hire an attractive housekeeper, fall in love with her, dump her, then walk on the beach with son and throw popcorn at him.

**Problem with Son**
Ex-wife and rich husband take him on a private jet to Mexico, and son thinks that he may like the new guy better than you.

**Mitch Solution**
When jet crashes into ocean, save his life and make new guy look like a coward.

**Problem with Son**
He's been having parties at your house without your permission.

**Mitch Solution**
Save him and his friends from the inevitable hang-gliding accident.

### ❓ Problem with Son
He misses his mom and wants you two to get married again.

### ❗ Mitch Solution
Propose to your ex-wife, show up at the wedding, then run away before exchanging vows because 'lives are in danger.'

### ❓ Problem with Son
He tells you that he's been having fantasies about a gorgeous woman on the beach.

### ❗ Mitch Solution
Tell him that 'nothing beats reality,' then prove it by flirting with the woman in front of him.

### ❓ Problem with Son
He's borrowed money from you to buy a skateboard, but instead he bought a synthesizer.

### ❗ Mitch Solution
Tell him that you always wanted to be a rock star too, then have an extended fantasy sequence in which you imagine what it would be like to be David Hasselhoff.

93

# THE BOOB FACTOR

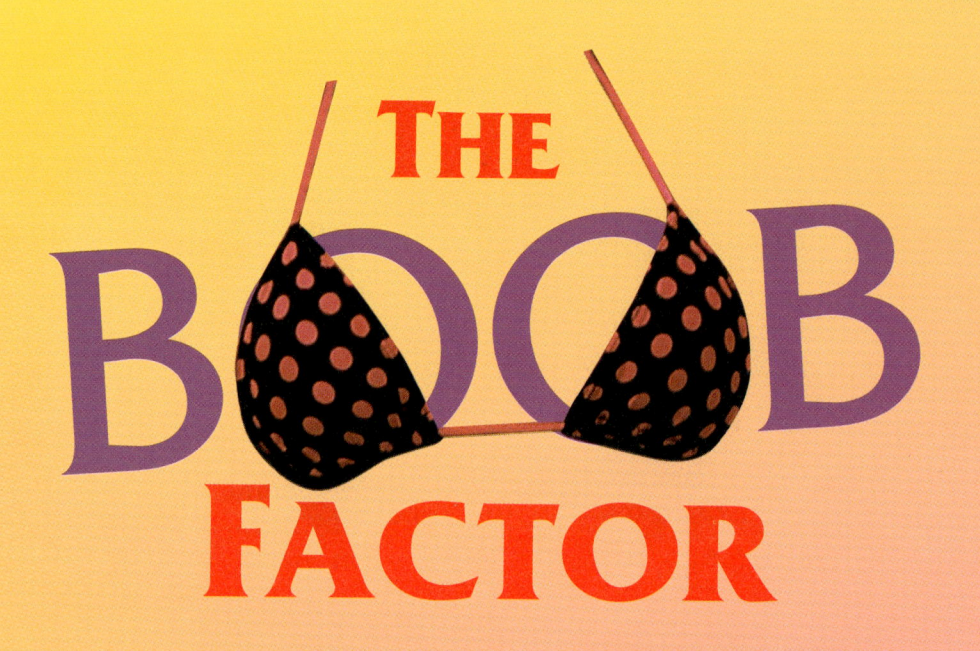

## Everything You Ever Wanted To Know About Baywatch Breasts … But Were Afraid To Ask

'Dow Corning, the largest maker of silicone breast implants, filed for bankruptcy today. In a related story, *Baywatch* stopped production.'

Jay Leno, *The Tonight Show*

There's no denying the obvious. Some of the most popular characters on *Baywatch* are breasts. And how could they not be? Those things are gorgeous, in an alienating sort of way. They aren't like normal, human breasts. They're huge, gravity-defying, perfectly tanned, man-made melons of majesty. Almost every *Baywatch* fan has a favorite set of *Baywatch* breasts, and it is impossible to watch the show and not be in awe of them. Those breasts are downright hypnotic.

The *Baywatch* breasts have become so legendary that they're easily as famous, if not *more* famous, than the actresses that wear them. If these breasts could speak, it's very likely that both Pamela Anderson Lee and Yasmine Bleeth would be written out of the scripts. Stories of *Baywatch* breast activity both on and off the set have dominated much of the press coverage of *Baywatch*, and the interest in these multi-faceted, mesmerizing mammaries shows no signs of fading. The *Baywatch* breasts will live in human imagination for the foreseeable future, and the artifacts themselves will probably still be perky and pert long after their owners are buried.

How much do you know about the *Baywatch* breast traditions? See if you can identify which of the following news bytes are real, and which are completely fabricated.

1. Pamela Anderson Lee and Yasmine Bleeth have contracts stipulating that they show a minimum of 15 cleavage close-ups per episode, basically one breast shot every four minutes.

*Ask not for whom the Baywatch breasts toll. They toll for thee!*

2. Nicole Eggert was fired from *Baywatch* because, according to Hasselhoff, 'Her breasts just weren't big enough.'
3. Alexandra Paul announced at a press conference that she was the first female actor on *Baywatch* 'with small breasts.'

*eph tries to hide her envy of C.J.'s love bumpers.*

4. *Baywatch* regular Gregory Alan-Williams told *Entertainment Tonight* that the only reason he's stayed with *Baywatch* for over six seasons is because, 'I love those big, bouncy boobies!'
5. The *Baywatch* writers were instructed never to use the word 'breast' on the programme, but instead to substitute the words 'bosoms,' 'love bumpers' or 'thingees.'

*Pam accepts her Golden Globes Award.*

6. David Hasselhoff has claimed in numerous interviews that he is opposed to blatant displays of breasts in *Baywatch*. 'I was always the one who fought against that stuff,' said David. 'I said we don't need to shoot cleavage any more and if you have one more long, lingering shot that is tasteless of a woman's breasts or of thong bikinis, then I'm leaving the show.'

7. In an episode of *Baywatch* when a boobacious guest star burst from a leather cat-suit, Hasselhoff admitted, 'The first thing I thought was, "She has nice breasts."'
8. Hasselhoff's wife, actress Pamela Bach, has never been invited to be a regular cast member on *Baywatch* because, according to Hasselhoff, 'Her breasts are just not *Baywatch* worthy.'
9. Pamela Anderson Lee spent more than two-thirds of the income from posing for *Playboy* to get her breasts enlarged, going from a 34C to a staggering 36D.
10. In Kenya, *Baywatch* is known as 'Beach of Talking Breasts.'
11. Pamela Anderson Lee has a suit specially designed to show off more cleavage.

12. The *Baywatch* Production Company nixed an episode just days before it was set to go into pre-production. The episode told the story of a visiting lifeguard who suffered from giganticism of the breasts.

13. Gena Lee Nolan claims that she wouldn't have gotten the part on *Baywatch* if she didn't have breast implants. She insists that getting a bigger bust was the turning point in her career.

> My agent says we're bigger than Laurel and Hardy

14. Former *Baywatch* actress Erika Elaniek said that she quit the show because she was having nightmares about her breasts, which were 'Whispering threats to me and claiming to be the *real* stars of *Baywatch*.'

15. Pamela Anderson Lee told *TV Guide* that most people think she 'can't stand next to a radiator or I'll melt.' She claimed this was not true, which implies that her chest modifications have been made heat-resistant.

(Answers: 1, 3, 6, 7, 9, 11, 13 and 15 are real *Baywatch* boob facts)

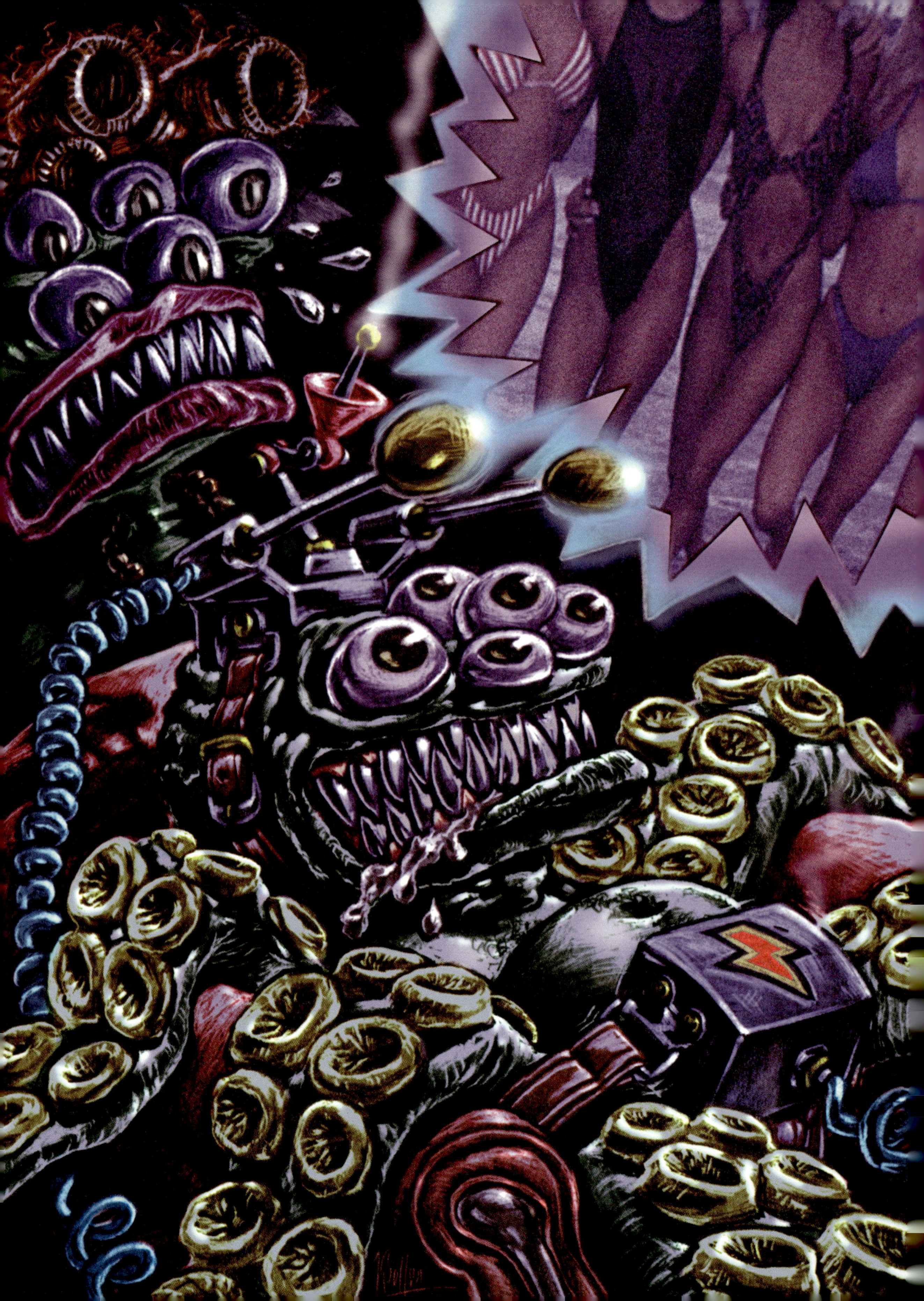

# MARS NEEDS WOMEN

### and Alpha Centauri would appreciate tapes of the fourth season

Little green men. Bulbous-headed cattle mutilators. The feathered serpent god Quetzalcoatl in a breathing helmet. Whatever form you imagine aliens take, they sure as hell know what you look like, as we've been sending pictures into the cosmos for over sixty years. Some scientists debate whether it's a good idea to tell other civilizations about this nice blue planet we got here, but the argument is moot.

Since our broadcasts move at the speed of light, the multi-tentacular folks at Alpha Centauri are taking in the opener of *Baywatch*'s third season ('River of No Return: Part One') right about … now. Further out, around Sirius, they haven't gotten into *Baywatch* yet, since they're just now catching our 1987 programming. So it's a sure bet they're grooving on *Cosby* and *Cheers*, and it's just as likely that they'll be big *Baywatch* fans in a couple of years, assuming they watch television, and assuming they're intelligent, and assuming there's life, which sort of means there must be planets around Sirius, and we aren't terribly certain about that, now that you mention it.

But knocking aside all of these things we have to assume before we can talk about aliens, let's tackle the big question: are there terrible bug-eyed monsters who dribble slime and want our women?

To be frank, we don't know. But it's a safe bet that if they do exist, they're into *Baywatch*. Or at the least, they will be just as soon as our broadcasts reach them.

There are heretical groups of scientists who believe that life began on Earth because of alien intervention. And according to a recent Gallup poll, more young Americans believe in UFOs than believe they'll get any state-sponsored retirement benefits.

What all of these people fail to realize is that it is equally likely that life was artificially created on Earth for the sole purpose of broadcasting *Baywatch* into the universe. Yes, our entire civilization may be nothing more

99

than the by-product of a massive effort by bug-eyed monsters to improve their viewing material.

This may sound far-fetched, but consider the top five reasons hideous, slimy alien beings probably enjoy *Baywatch*:

1. The whole thing views like a live-action menu, without pesky clothes to distract from meat quality.
2. No methane beaches!
3. Since humans come in only two genders, they can actually follow the romances.
4. Yasmine Bleeth is much perkier than the hive-queen.
5. The women never decapitate the men after sex, as in those disturbing sit-coms coming from Andromeda.

There is, however, a downside. If drippy, slimy alien beings created us for the sole purpose of providing them *Baywatch*, it may not go well for us when we finally cancel the series. There will be a time-delay, of course, since it will take years for the final episode to reach them. But let's remember that Alpha Centauri is only 4.3 light years behind us. So if *Baywatch* were to be canceled tomorrow, in exactly 4.3 years they'd be polishing their jackboots on Alpha Centauri.

No, we'd better all hope that the squishy, horrible alien things who may or may not be rabid *Baywatch* fans are somewhere in the galactic core, which is over 30,000 light years away. If that is the case, we have about thirty more millennia to come up with something as good as *Baywatch*, or face global annihilation.

Peoples of Earth, pay heed: bring back *Knight Rider* or perish.

**Intelligent life across the galaxy agree: 'We sure do love them boobies'**

# Are there terrible bug-eyed monsters who dribble slime and want our women?

# Reading Between the Lines

Most of the dialogue on *Baywatch* sounds so silly and moronic that it may lead you to believe that the lifeguards (or the writers) are idiots. This is not so. We examined a few classic *Baywatch* lines to see if we could find deeper meanings hidden in the seemingly shallow words. We were not disappointed.

**What They Say**

I came here to have fun, and I'm not having fun any more

**What They Mean**

The world is a scary, unpredictable place. You will not always enjoy it

**What They Say**

I just wanna be nasty and play with my hair

**What They Mean**

Sometimes the simple things in life are the most pleasurable

**What They Say**

That's kind of a neat idea – I've never been to a hurricane party

**What They Mean**

Make the best of every situation, no matter how disastrous it might seem at first

**What They Say**

You are one taco short of a combination

**What They Mean**

Your blatant disregard for logic and reason disturbs me

**What They Say**

It's the Hawaiian Dance of Desire. Come, let me teach you

**What They Mean**

A multi-cultural education is essential in these politically correct days

**What They Say**

That's 'Mr Dude' to you

**What They Mean**

Structure is important, even in an informal atmosphere

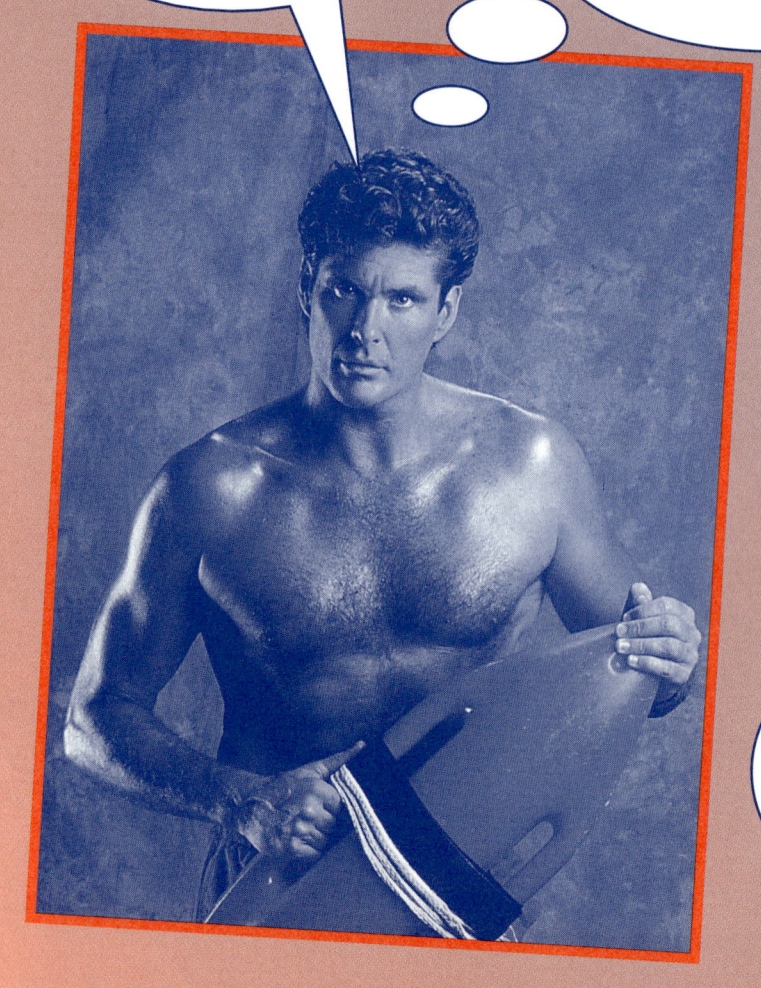

**What They Say**

There's been, like, no waves all day

**What They Mean**

Nature is a powerful force that adheres to its own rules, and it will not always cooperate with our wishes

**What They Say**

Just look at this body. And look at these muscles. So many of them, all in one place

**What They Mean**

The human body is a rich tapestry of tissues and organs, and should be appreciated

**What They Mean**

Life is filled with bountiful opportunity. What you do not accomplish today you can do tomorrow

**What They Say**

If you'd rather go jogging than surf-skiing, no problemo

# Stephanie's BAD DATES

Stephanie may know a thing or two about lifeguarding, but she doesn't know jack about men. During her four-year career at *Baywatch*, she has never had even *one* successful relationship with a man. This is because most of her dates start out wonderfully, and then end in total disaster. We're not talking about rejection, we mean guns and fires and almost certain death. Why does Stephanie have such incredibly bad luck when it comes to men? We don't have an answer for that, but if Stephanie has taught us anything, it's that there is no such thing as a 'harmless' first date.

**The Wonderful Start**
Stephanie and Mitch have a romantic rendezvous on a private yacht.

**THE HORRIFYING FINISH**
Pirates board their yacht, tie them up and threaten to kill them if they don't empty their bank accounts.

**The Wonderful Start**
Stephanie has a picnic on the beach with a sexy doctor.

**THE HORRIFYING FINISH**
The doctor notices a cancerous mole on the back of her leg and tells her that she's going to die.

**The Wonderful Start**
Stephanie and Mitch work a 24-hour Call Car shift and rekindle their affections for each other.

**THE HORRIFYING FINISH**
Mitch's son, Hobie, gets into a hang gliding accident and Mitch ditches her to go save him.

'Doctor, they've filled my air ring with helium.'

106

BAYWATCH
JUSTICE LEAGUE
FORCES OF EVIL
BEWARE!
ZACHARY PRESENT

IT'S ANOTHER DAY ON THE BEACH IN SUNNY CALIFORNIA, AND THE BAYWATCH JUSTICE LEAGUE IS THERE TO PROTECT THE LIFE & LIBERTY OF ALL IT'S CITIZENS.

BUT SUDDENLY...

HELP!

MITCH AND HIS TE... OF SUPER-LIFEGUAR... SPRING TO ACTIO... PULLING THE DROWNI... VICTIM TO SAFET...

MY DANGER SENSE IS TINGLING — GOTTA STAY SHARP

AFTER PERFORMING CPR AND COMPLETING THE NECESSARY PAPERWORK, THEY DISCOVER THAT THE VICTIM IS FORMER ISRAELI PRIME MINISTER SHIMON PERES!

THANKS FOR SAVING MY LIFE, MITCH.

ANY TIME, SHIMON.

PERES EXPLAINS THAT HE WAS TAKING A SWIM TO TAKE HIS MIND OFF TERRORISM IN THE MIDDLE EAST.

THERE'S A U.N. MEETING TODAY TO DISCUSS THE MATTER. HOPEFULLY WE CAN FIND A WAY TO LIVE TOGETHER IN PEACE.

MITCH REALIZES THAT HIS JOB IS NOT YET DONE.

THIS IS AN OUTRAGE!

MIND IF WE TAG ALONG?

NICE PECS!

UNITED NATION

LATER THAT NIGHT, THE U.N. COUNCIL IS IN AN UPROAR OVER THE APPEARANCE OF THE BAYWATCH JUSTICE LEAGUE.

PEACE IN THE MIDDLE EAST
1) C.P.R.
2) BAYWATCH JUSTICE LEAGUE

I REMEMBER A TIME WHEN LOGAN & BRODY HAD A DISAGREEMENT. I MADE THEM TAKE A CANOE TRIP AND THEY WORKED EVERYTHING OUT.

MITCH ADDRESSES THE COUNCIL AND OFFERS HIS ADVICE ON STOPPING TERRORISM.

TO BE CONTINUED.

| | |
|---|---|
| THE COUNCIL IS CONVINCED. "FASCINATING CONCEPT" "BY JIFFY IT JUST COULD WORK!" | MEANWHILE, THE FRENCH PRIME MINISTER LURES C.J. INTO THE BASEMENT AND ATTEMPTS TO SEDUCE HER. "HAVE YOU EVER BEEN TO PARIS?" "THERE ARE NO BEACHES IN PARIS YO SILLY FOO" |
| SHE SEES A SHADOWY FIGURE IN THE DISTANCE AND DECIDES TO CHECK IT OUT. "THIS DOESN'T LOOK GOOD" | SHE RECOGNIZES THE CULPRIT, HIZBOLLAH SECRETARY-GENERAL SHEIKH HASSAN NASRALLAH. "THIS BOMB WILL BLOW UP THE WATER PIPES AND DROWN THEM ALL. THEN, ISRAEL WILL BE MINE!" |
| C.J. CONTACTS LOGAN WITH HER TELEKINETIC POWERS "LOGAN, COME QUICKLY." "I'M ON MY WAY." | "NOT SO FAST, HASSAN!" WHAP "BLAST! IT'S THOSE DAMN BAYWATCHERS AGAIN!" |

BUT IT'S TOO LATE! THE BOMB GOES OFF AND THE U.N. MEETING IS FLOODED WITH WATER.
BOOOOOM
NICE WORK, CODY
THANKS, STEPHANIE
LUCKILY, THE BAYWATCH JUSTICE LEAGUE IS THERE TO SAVE THE DAY!
THE SHEIKH SEES THAT HE IS NO MATCH FOR THE BAY-WATCHERS AND GRUDGINGLY AGREES TO STOP THE FIGHTING IN THE MIDDLE EAST.
I'M PROUD OF YOU BOYS
THE FRENCH PRIME MINISTER DECIDES TO CHANGE HIS WAYS TOO.
NEVER AGAIN WILL I WASTE TAX-PAYERS TIME SEDUCING YOUNG BLONDE WOMEN. NOW, I STAND FOR FREEDOM AND BAYWATCH VALUES.
THAT'S THE SPIRIT LOVER
TO CELEBRATE, MITCH PUTS ON A ROCK SHOW, LAYING DOWN THE FUNKY JAMS FOR THE NEW WORLD ORDER.
KEEP HOLDING ON TO THE LIFELINE!
... A NEW WORLD ORDER FOR ALL!
THE END.

# The Ultimate BAYWATCH Trivia Quiz

So you think you know a thing or two about *Baywatch*, do you? Well, we'll just see about that. You may have seen every episode, and you may have read all the fan magazines and watched all the TV interviews. And maybe you've aced every *Baywatch* quiz that's come your way. But that doesn't give you the right to call yourself a *Baywatch* expert. Not yet, anyway.

If you really think you qualify as a scholar of all things *Baywatch*, then let's put that knowledge to the test. We challenge you to take the Ultimate *Baywatch* Trivia Quiz. We promise that it is unlike any trivia quiz you have ever taken before. There are no obvious or easy questions that any fool with half a brain and a TV remote could answer. This is the only *Baywatch* trivia quiz to focus on the really obscure and vague aspects of the show. It will separate the men from the boys, the women from the girls, the Mitch Buchannons from the John D. Corts.

So grab yourself a #2 pencil and find out once and for all if you really know anything about the most popular TV show in the world. We double-dog dare you.

1. Baywatch understands the importance of recycling. Film, that is. Which of the following scenes were used in more than one episode?
a. Mitch sees Stephanie undressing in the locker-room and nearly exposes himself.
b. A fat surfer with a rash asks C.J. to rub lotion on his back.
c. Mitch talks to a recently paralyzed buddy at the hospital.
d. C.J. stands on the beach, and the camera pans up from her ankles to her thighs to her hips to her boobs to her pouty face.
e. All of the above

*It's the old story: a fat guy, a bodacious babe and a nasty rash.*

2. Gregory Alan-Williams does more than play a goofy cop on *Baywatch* and *Baywatch Nights.* He's also a goofy public speaker and book author. He's traveled across the country, talking to students about racism and heroism (and promoting his books about racism and heroism). Which of the following deep thoughts by Master Williams is not authentic?
a. 'Say hey for T & A !'
b. 'Someone asked me not too long ago to share my thoughts on what was the greatest problem facing the country. I thought about it for a moment and answered, "Me." '
c. 'Racism ain't "phat." It ain't "kickin." If you're a racist, you're not down with me.'
d. 'It takes a lot of vegetables to make a stew, and if you had a stew that had nothing but potatoes, it would get pretty tedious.'

3. In 'The Trophy,' a teenage girl wants her friends to think that she's had sex with Eddie the lifeguard. What did she leave in his tower?
a. Her swimsuit
b. Her panties
c. Her backpack
d. Her hymen

4. In *People* magazine, how did cross-dressing fashion commentator RuPaul describe the evening gown Pamela Anderson Lee wore to the 1995 European Music Awards?
a. An altar to womanhood
b. A monument to sexual vibrancy
c. A Grecian temple
d. A bag full of dead puppies

> It takes a lot of vegetables to make a stew

*A bag full of dead puppies?*

*I like Ike*

7. In 'Island of Romance,' Mitch and Hobie interview housemaids, most of which are zany ethnic stereotypes. Which of the following stereotypes don't they meet?
a. A fat Indian woman
b. A Japanese Samurai
c. A Mexican guy wearing a huge sombrero
d. A big, black, southern-cookin' mama

*Mitch Buchannon, I've found a huge skid mark on your Y-fronts*

5. The *Baywatch* lifeguards have strong political opinions, but they are not always allowed to express them. According to the *Baywatch* Lifeguard Manual, which of the following restrictions are not enforced on politically-minded Baywatchers?
a. A lifeguard may not use official authority to influence an election.
b. Partisanship may not be shown while in uniform.
c. Political campaign literature is not allowed in any lifeguard facilities.
d. A lifeguard may not vote for any candidate who is overweight or 'tubby'.

6. *Baywatch* has been broadcast in India for over two years. What did Amita Malik, the nation's most prominent television critic, suggest that the program symbolizes?
a. 'The possibility of a world united in peace and harmony.'
b. 'The sheer health of American youth.'
c. 'Tasty thighs and scrumptious buttocks.'
d. 'Further proof of the transcendent power of Shiva.'

*Tasty thighs and scrumptious buttocks or further proof of the transcendent power of Shiva?*

"What do you call a man with half a brain?"

"Gifted!"

8. Hollywood's paparazzi have managed to expose almost every aspect of Pamela Anderson Lee's life, but they have not yet been able to invade her dreams. Which of the following images has not been recorded in one of Pam's dream journals?
a. Four rows of woman, naked from the waist down, praying to Buddha.
b. Her breasts become wise-cracking comedians who put down her career choices.
c. Tommy Lee driving a tiny Lego car.
d. She's in a mental institution with Anna Nicole Smith, who's hooked up to an IV drip unit.

9. When David Hasselhoff was a guest on the *Tonight Show*, he claimed that he was on TV so often that one of his employees was unable to make love to his wife. Who was the employee?
a. His pool guy
b. His accountant
c. His maid
d. His personal secretary

10. Because they spend so much screen time in bathing suits, it's important that the *Baywatch* actors keep in shape. Match the name of the actor or actress with their official *Baywatch* weight.

| | |
|---|---|
| a. Pamela Anderson Lee | 1. 108 pounds |
| b. Erika Eleniak | 2. 117 pounds |
| c. David Hasselhoff | 3. 105 pounds |
| d. Yasmine Bleeth | 4. 195 pounds |

11. David Hasselhoff has found international success as a pop-rock performer, in part because of the painfully tight pants he wears during his live concerts. According to Hasselhoff, how many octaves higher do his pants force him to sing?
a. One octave
b. Two octaves
c. Five octaves
d. Eighteen octaves

"These pants are like a cheap hotel …"

"… there's no ballroom"

*Can marrying this man prevent shark attacks?*

13. When four fifteen-foot sharks were sighted swimming dangerously close to the *Baywatch* set, what did Pamela Anderson Lee do to protect herself?
a. Put on a pair of sheepskin boots.
b. Doused her body with 'Shark-B-Gone' shark repellent.
c. Instructed her stunt double to go into the water for her.
d. Married rocker Tommy Lee.

14. According to *Baywatch*, which of the following qualities do fat people not possess?
a. Honor
b. Integrity
c. Beauty
d. Talent
e. All of the above

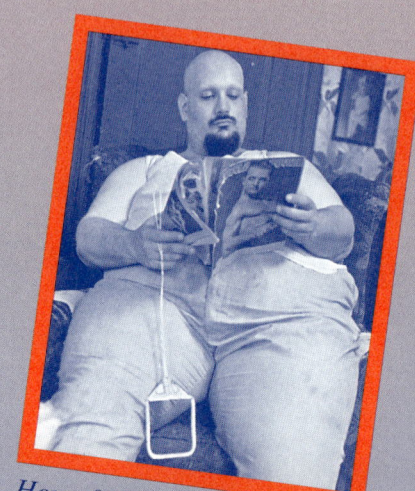

*'Oh for a cleavage-free world.'*

12. In 'Home is Where the Heat Is,' what did Stephanie reveal to be 'one of life's great quandaries'?
a. Can you love a man even though you know he's a jewel thief?
b. Protect your feelings or let yourself be vulnerable?
c. Save a young boy from drowning or let the little sod go under?
d. Devote your life to what you love or find a job where you don't have to expose so much cleavage?

*Honor? Integrity? Beauty? Are you kidding?*

116

*Boobies, boobies, boobies!*

**15.** In 'K-Gas: The Groove Yard of Solid Gold,' Chicago comic Jeff Garlin guest stars as an embezzling radio DJ who falls in love with C.J. Parker. What was the name of Garlin's 1991 one-man show in Chicago, and how much did the tickets cost?
a. 'I Want Someone To Eat Cheese With,' $10
b. 'Boobies, Boobies, Boobies,' $40
c. 'Hey, I'm a Fat Guy!' $25
d. 'Shortsighted,' $15

**16.** If *Baywatch* could be represented as a chemical compound – albumin, for instance – which comprises a chain of amino acids composed of carbon, hydrogen and nitrogen, then what would be its 'molecular' weight?
a. 34,000
b. 70,000
c. 152,000
d. 36 D cup

*What's your molecular weight?*

*36 D cup*

**ANSWERS:** (Give yourself 2 points for each correct answer)
1:e, 2:c, 3:a, 4:c, 5:d, 6:b, 7:c, 8:b, 9:a, 10:(a-3, b-1, c-4, d-2), 11:b, 12:b, 13:a, 14:e, 15:a, 16:d.

**SCORING**:

**0-8:** Listen punk, regardless of what you may think, you don't know diddley about *Baywatch*. You've got a lot of nerve calling yourself a *Baywatch* fan, because you definitely are not. You probably think that Summer Quinn is a type of suntan lotion, don't you? Moron. Go back and do your homework and stop wasting our time.

**10-16:** OK, so you have a limited knowledge of *Baywatch*, but don't get cocky. You still have a lot to learn and you could probably stand to watch another hundred episodes or so. But pay attention this time. Lazy viewing will not be tolerated.

**18-24:** You're well on your way to completing your *Baywatch* education. You know your way around a scarab and could probably intelligently discuss the differences between a man o' war and a jellyfish. But remember to continue watching and studying the show, as you are still missing some key elements. We'd suggest watching episodes frame-by-frame to pick up on the subtler qualities of *Baywatch*.

**26-32:** *Baywatch* is in your blood. You live, breathe, eat and shit the show. Not many people know as much about *Baywatch* as you do, and frankly, that scares us. We didn't really think anybody would be able to answer all of these questions. It was a joke. But apparently the joke's on us. OK then, we'll back off. You are clearly 'The Man.' You might want to consider taking some time away from *Baywatch* for a while. Maybe read a book or leave the house. This obsession can't be healthy. Just a thought.

# BAYWATCH
## Tool of the CIA?

transcript: begin tape
CIA Guy: You aren't taping this call, are you?
Planet *Baywatch*: No, no, I'm just taking notes.
CIA Guy: Good. Things are fairly tense right now, with the Senate hearings.
P.B: I appreciate your willingness to talk, period.
CIA Guy: So you want to know about *Baywatch*?
P.B: Yeah. Does your agency have any involvement with the show?

CIA Guy: What do you mean by 'involvement'?
P.B: Seems like a simple question to me. Is your agency interested in *Baywatch*, and are you involved with the show on any level?
CIA Guy: No comment.
P.B: Oh, come on.
CIA Guy: Sorry. No comment.
P.B: Hmm. OK, how does your agency feel about *Baywatch*?
CIA Guy: We're very pleased, of course.
P.B: Why 'of course'?
CIA Guy: *Baywatch* is spreading our culture across the globe. There are places we've been trying to hit for years, with

limited success, and then suddenly - presto! - there's a show doing it for us.

P.B: And that's as far as it goes?

CIA Guy: What do you mean?

P.B: Admit it: you're in touch with the producers, aren't you?

CIA Guy: You've got to be kidding.

PB: Are you denying that you approve scripts?

CIA Guy: What?

P.B: Word on the street is that *Baywatch* is CIA to the core, that nothing happens without a greenlight from Langley, and that the only reason they've broken into so many foreign markets is that your agency and the State Department have been strong-arming the Third World with threats of embargoes and assassinations.

*pause*

CIA Guy: That's the stupidest thing I ever heard. You're ...

P.B: Are you willing to confirm that *Baywatch* is run by U.S. intelligence?

CIA Guy: What I'm trying to ...

P.B: So who exactly are the CIA people on the show?

CIA Guy: Nobody!

P.B: You're just saying that to protect your people. I understand.

CIA Guy: I was trying to say ... just hang on for a minute, OK? I was trying to make a real point. It really does aid U.S. interests to have our culture represented globally. But *Baywatch* is just a part of that.

P.B: A big part.

CIA Guy: Yes, very big.

P.B: And the part that you directly control.

CIA Guy: Lay off of that, will you?

P.B: Why? Because we're so close to the truth? Because you

don't want us exposing the fact that you run the show?
**CIA Guy: It's been nice talking to you.**
P.B: Do you deny that it was CIA funding that rescued the show from its original cancellation?
**CIA Guy: Goodbye.**
P.B: We're going to blow this whole thing wide open:

*dial tone*

P.B: Hello? Hello? Hello?

*end tape*

CIA deny involvement with Baywatch *but here agents keep a close eye on Pammie's movements.*

# PECS of the Stars

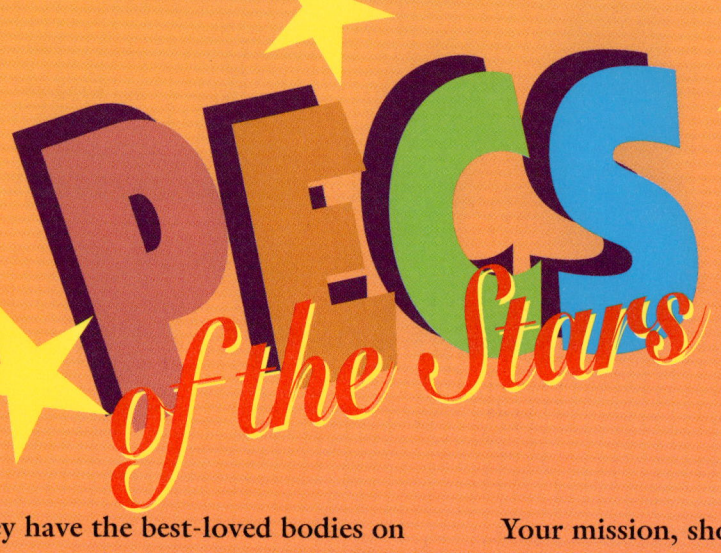

Since they have the best-loved bodies on the planet, you should be able to tell them apart without looking at their faces (in other words, cheating).

Your mission, should you choose to accept it: identify the chests below, and sort them out from the non-*Baywatch* nipples we've mixed in.

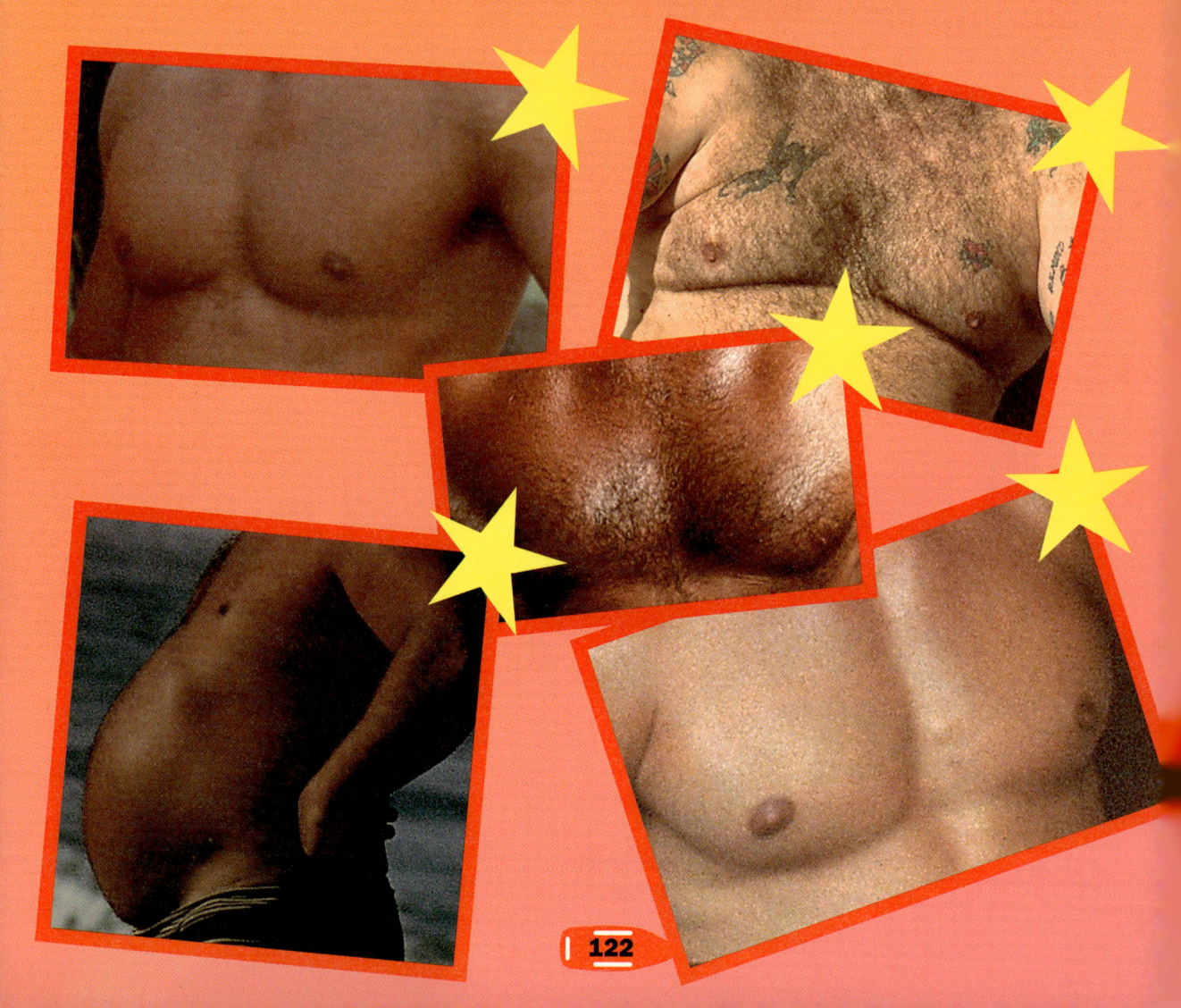

123

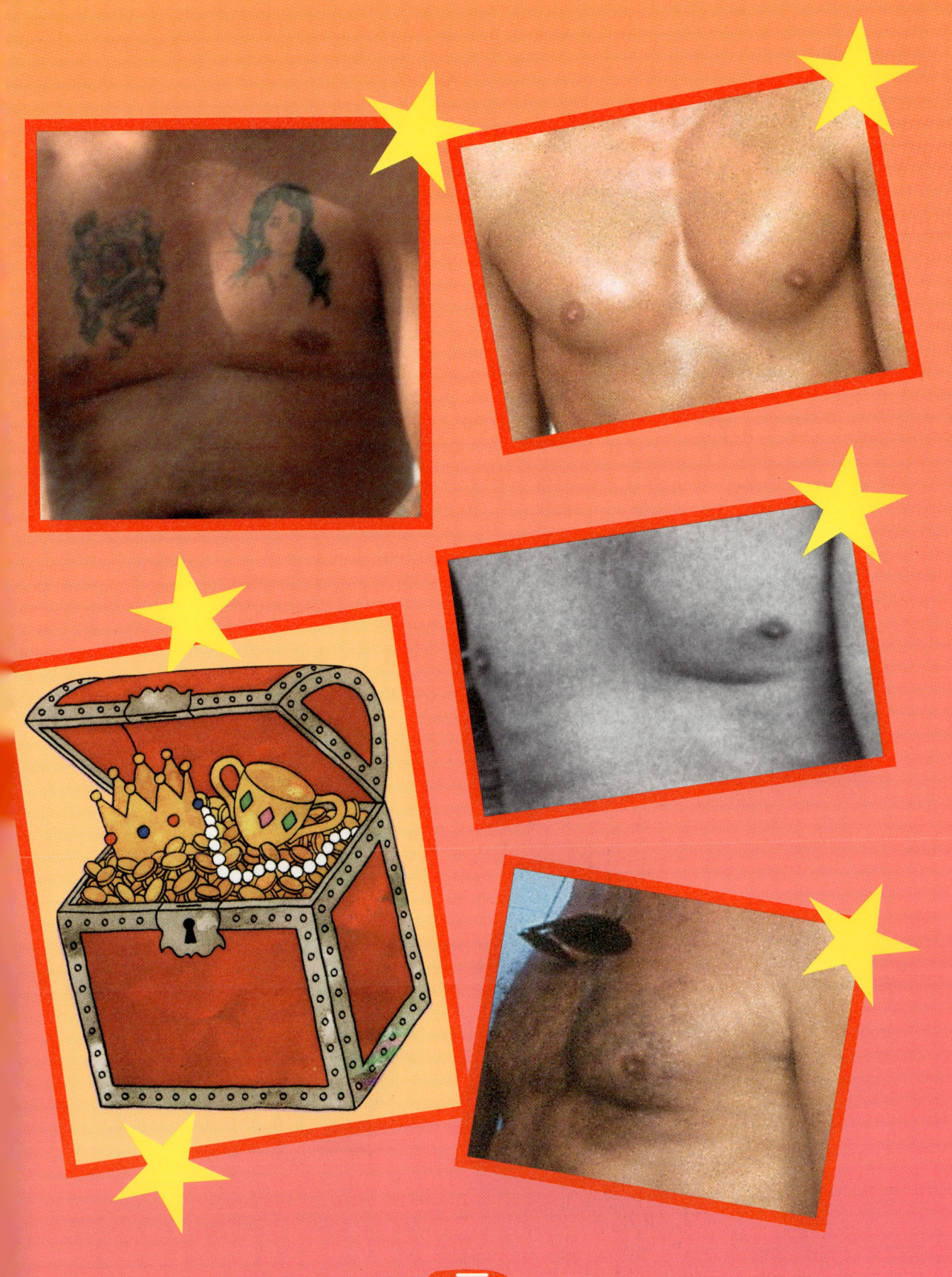

# Postscript

– or –

## Why *Baywatch* is Exactly Like Joseph Conrad's *Heart of Darkness*

WE LIED THROUGH OUR TEETH when *Playboy* offered the job. '*Baywatch*?' Spitzy said into the phone, 'sure, we've seen it, and we'd love to write something about it. You betcha. No problem. Two weeks? Can do!' I suppose our editor knew we were full of shit, but that's how it goes sometimes. You don't have to tell the truth when you're a satirist, so long as your lies are amusing and unconfirmable.

I panicked when I heard the news. 'How are we going to get tapes?' I demanded. 'There's no way the distributor will give us whole seasons, and the show's already been on for, what, *five* seasons? We're dead! We're meat! We're history!'

Spitzy tried to calm me down, but all that evening I was prone to sudden fits of moaning. We made calls to various people in Los Angeles, but the answer didn't change: no tapes. Eventually Spitzy gave up trying to wrestle the bottle of whiskey away from me, and joined me in a few shots.

By the time my roommate got home, I was a drunken mess. I tearfully explained to him that we had accepted an assignment from *Playboy* that we were completely unqualified for. How could we write humorous commentary on a show we'd never seen? Of course the show was huge, and of course we knew plenty of people who'd seen it, but what the hell good was that? You can't write comedy off second-hand impressions. You need the real thing for mockery.

As it turned out, he had a friend who was a real *Baywatch* fanatic. This guy, David Sparks, taped the show regularly and had whole folders of press clippings about all things David Hasselhoffian. He'd even hosted a local radio program called 'The *Baywatch* Report,' where he'd review episodes and discuss the show in depth.

The next day, armed with David Sparks's address, Spitzy and I marched to his apartment. David buzzed us into his front door, and eyed us with open suspicion, which was fair, as we're fairly suspicious-looking guys. I hadn't been eating too well, since writing pays sporadically, and my shaved head did nothing to hide my red eyes and gaunt features. Spitzy was dressed in some nightmare parody of motley, and gave the distinct impression of a clown on amyl nitrate. From the get-go, David regretted letting us into his home.

He puttered around his clean little apartment, muttering things like, 'You know, if anybody should be writing this article, it's me.' I asked him repeatedly about where he was keeping his tapes, but he deflected my questions, changing the subject. While he was busy in the kitchen making tea, Spitzy and I huddled for a conference. What could we do if he wouldn't give us the tapes?

'We could beat him up,' Spitzy whispered. 'We're both bigger than him.'

This was true. David seemed like the kind of guy who would go down crying if you popped him a quick one on the nose. It might work. 'But what if we can't find the tapes?' I hissed. 'What if they're in storage?'

Before we could take this any farther, David returned with his tea. 'I'm the real *Baywatch* expert,' he declared, slamming his cup down so that Earl Grey sloshed over the rim. 'You guys haven't even seen an episode.'

We nodded dutifully.

'And do you know how long it's taken me to put this library together?' he said, waving toward his bedroom. *That must be where the tapes are*, I thought. *Gotcha*. 'I've been into *Baywatch* since its first season on network television — since before it was syndicated!'

We nodded dutifully.

The afternoon wore on in a strange sort of journalistic Mexican standoff. David wouldn't give us the tapes, and we wouldn't leave, despite his pointed hints. Finally he relented enough to show us a montage he'd put together, mixing shots of David Hasselhoff with the big operatic death scene from *Platoon*, where the sergeant raises his hands to heaven as he's riddled with bullets. 'You see?' he demanded. 'Hasselhoff is making this big *Platoon* reference, which is a reference to Christ. Don't you see?'

As night fell, I was beginning to agree with Spitzy. We could take this guy. And I was increasingly convinced that the tapes were in his bedroom. Hell, we wouldn't even have to bloody his nose; Spitzy could hold him while I snatched his library, and we'd be out of the apartment before he could call for help. What would he tell the police, anyway? Please officer, help me, these two thugs stole my *Baywatch* tapes? After all, this was the big city, and people probably stole *Baywatch* episodes all the time. If there was no blood, there'd be no investigation. We'd get away with it scot-free.

Although he hadn't said anything, I could tell Spitzy was ready. He was shifting toward the edge of his seat, flexing his hands. I moved my legs under me so I could spring at David as soon as my partner made his move.

'Well,' David sighed over his now-cold tea, 'I suppose I could loan a few of them to you for a little while.'

Spitzy relaxed. I shifted my feet out from under my body. 'How long could we have them?' I asked, a forced smile on my face.

'When's your article due?'

'Two months,' I lied. 'We'll need the tapes for at least that long.'

David looked like he'd been sucking a lemon. 'Well …'

'We'll see if we can get you a free subscription to *Playboy*,' Spitzy volunteered. 'I think they'd do that.' We both knew this was patently false, so I agreed.

Before long, David had a small box full of tapes out in the living room. 'You'll take good care of them?' he asked.

'Sure, sure,' I said, peering back toward his bedroom. 'That stack over there, are those *Baywatch* tapes, too?'

Grudgingly, David nodded. A little more pressure, and he'd filled a large sack with videocassettes. 'Two months, right?'

We were already out the door, headed down the steps. 'Sure thing,' Spitzy called over his shoulder. 'We'll have 'em back in no time at all.' When we hit the street, I looked back at David's building. For a fleeting moment I glimpsed his face in the window, and it looked as though he were crying.

It was the height of Chicago's Killer Summer, and temperatures were hovering around 100 degrees Fahrenheit. By the end of the heatwave, more than 250 people would be dead from heat exposure. We were both sweating through our clothes by the time we made it back to my apartment, which was utterly without luxuries such as air-conditioning. Night should have made things cooler, but somehow didn't.

Doing my best to avoid dripping sweat on to the tapes, I stacked them next to my television. 'We'll make another pile over here,' I pointed, 'of the ones we've seen.' As I shoveled tape after tape out of the sack, Spitzy's eyes grew wide.

'There's no way we'll get through all of those in time,' he blurted out.

'Not unless we start now. For the next week we are going to live, breathe, and eat *Baywatch*.' I slapped a cassette at random into the VCR, and hit the rewind button. 'Grab a notebook.'

For the first twelve hours we were OK. We wrote down jokes and snippets, exchanged ideas, and were generally productive little writer boys. We broke off long after dawn and crossed the street to Manny's Diner for breakfast. 'Let's get a little sleep,' Spitzy suggested, 'and start up again.'

For the next round we arranged a couple of fans in my living room, which didn't help at all. When the air reaches a certain critical point of heat and humidity, fans just make it feel like there's a great big dog licking your body. Although we were both becoming dangerously dehydrated, we stayed glued to our chairs, soaking in every detail we could glean about *Baywatch*.

'For the next week we are going to live, breathe and eat Baywatch.'

In the middle of the second night I noticed that we'd both stopped writing in our notebooks. We had crossed over from talking about the show as subject matter, and were instead discussing the characters and their development.

'This one must be first season,' Spitzy commented. 'Stephanie has long hair.'

'Yeah,' I said. 'I like her better with short hair.'

We both nodded, notebooks forgotten.

Just before dawn we collapsed, and as I tossed and turned on sweat-stained sheets, I heard the opening song from *Baywatch*. For a moment I thought that Spitzy was watching tapes without me. By the time I'd struggled out of bed, I realized that it was just my imagination. As I lay back down, I again heard the strains of 'I'm Always Here,' and it rocked me to sleep like a mother's gentle hands.

On the third day we were starting to crack. We were less than a quarter of the way through the tapes, and the heat was making us edgy and violent. We began to cut each other's ideas down, and suddenly nothing was very funny, and if we didn't have this article done in time, it would probably be the other guy's fault, dammit. Despite the heat, I began to drink. 'Oh yeah,' Spitzy sneered, 'that'll make you funnier.'

By two a.m. I had given up on writing, and was sinking into an orange fog of *Baywatch* and whiskey. Sweat was pouring down my face, and I had to mop my forehead frequently, or stinging beads of salt-laced sweat would drip into my eyes. The temperature was reported to be 104, and the death toll was all anyone could talk about on the radio. I realized that my partner had been talking for some time, and I hadn't heard a word.

*A journey into the darkest heart of America ...*

'I mean, I just don't know,' he said, voice cracking. 'Is this the best way to write an article? I ... I mean ... I ... what are we doing!?'

'Juss watch the tapes,' I slurred.

'No, no, I won't just watch the tapes! I don't think — I mean, I'm not — I mean, we're not doing it the right way, I don't think. How much have we really written? The article's due in a few days, and and and and we're just sitting here watching I mean we've been at this for three straight days now and we're nowhere near done and look at that pile of tapes my God we're barely halfway through and I DON'T KNOW HOW MUCH MORE OF THIS I CAN TAKE!'

In my heart I agreed with him, but this had become bigger than us, bigger than the article, bigger even than *Playboy*. We were on a journey into the darkest heart of America, home of the brave, and we couldn't possibly stop halfway through. No, we were going to sit through every episode of *Baywatch* if it killed us, only it wouldn't, and we'd emerge out the other side glowing like some Nietzschean dream of will, and we'd be better men for it; stronger, tougher, more powerful. Awestruck mortals would ask us why we did it, and we'd look at them and answer, 'Because it was there.' And I knew this wasn't heat exhaustion muddling my brain — we had found our calling, our purpose, our challenge.

I gestured limply at the television. 'The tapes stay on,' I said with what I hoped sounded like finality. I took another swig from the bottle. Spitzy didn't seem to have heard me. He was looking for the remote control. I hid it under a stack of paper while he scrabbled around the coffee table.

Spitzy was fiddling with my VCR, but it was one of those weird ones where there are no controls on the front, and if you lose the remote you're screwed.

'Where's the remote!?' he said, turning on me.

I shrugged.

'Brendan,' he said, pointing an accusing finger in my direction, 'this isn't working and we have to turn it off! Turn it off! Turn it off!'

Shaking my head, I set the bottle down and shoved it across the floor at him. 'The tapes stay on.'

He collapsed back on to the sofa, defeated. His eyes were wide with desperation. To placate him temporarily, I picked up my notebook and doodled around with a pen. Convinced that I was doing something productive, he quieted down, and began to drink heavily.

I have no memory of turning off the VCR, but we must have, since we ate and slept. We were rapidly losing track of time. Was this day four or five? Neither of us knew.

At some indeterminate point my roommate came home from work. 'Jesus Christ,' he said, 'are you guys *still* watching *Baywatch*?'

We looked up from our seats, hollow-eyed and hunched. '*Baywatch*,' Spitzy said.

'*Baywatch*,' I agreed.

My roommate fled to his room and would not come out. Throughout the night we would begin chanting, '*Baywatch* ... Baaaaywatch ... Baaaaaaywaaaaatch ...' in hopes that he would join us on our journey. He never did.

Whatever tenuous grip on space and time I had was lost. I know I slept, and I know that the sun rose and fell several times. Once, when I fell asleep, instead of hearing the main theme song, all I could hear was the closing music. This made me very happy. Spitzy had not spoken in a long while, but that was OK. We didn't need words any more. We had *Baywatch*.

And then, without any warning, there were no more tapes on the *To Watch* pile. Spitzy looked confused, but I was nearly paralyzed. For six or seven days our world had consisted of nothing but those tapes — how could they be gone? Where could we get more? For most of that morning we tottered around my apartment, shaky as new-foaled colts. Spitzy left in the afternoon to spend time with his girlfriend. I figured he had the right idea, and called up a girl I knew, hoping I could use sex and sweat to get *Baywatch* out of my system.

After this brief respite, we got down to the serious business of writing the article. We had begun to speak again, which was probably a good thing. I was feeling weak but proud, like a man who had killed a bull rhinoceros with his bare hands. No, more like Luke must have felt after he went into the grotto that Yoda told him was strong in the dark side of the Force, and he chopped Darth Vader's head off, only it was his own, and it was all very Freudian and deep. Yeah, that's how I felt. And what's more, I had made it through without cracking up. How many hours of *Baywatch* had we subjected ourselves to? Ninety? A hundred? More?

Chest out, chin in, I strutted around the apartment, convinced that I was the psychic equivalent of Clint Eastwood, John Wayne and Mel Gibson, only rolled up into one and turned blonde. *Yeah*, I thought, *I'm as tough as they come*. I felt the pride that abused women are said to feel, the I-could-take-it-without-breaking sense of empowerment.

Spitzy was using my phone to call our agent. When he got off, he looked strangely thoughtful. 'I don't know how to tell you this,' he said.

'What?'

'That was our agent.'

'I know.'

'She thinks we ought to do a book on *Baywatch*.' He paused to let this sink in. 'It'll mean watching a lot more episodes. What do you think?'

Suddenly I was on my knees in the hall, and for no reason I could explain I was slamming my fists into the floor over and over again. 'Damn you!' I screamed, although who I was cursing I couldn't say. '*Damn you all to hell!*'

He says I was weeping, but I think it was just the sweat.

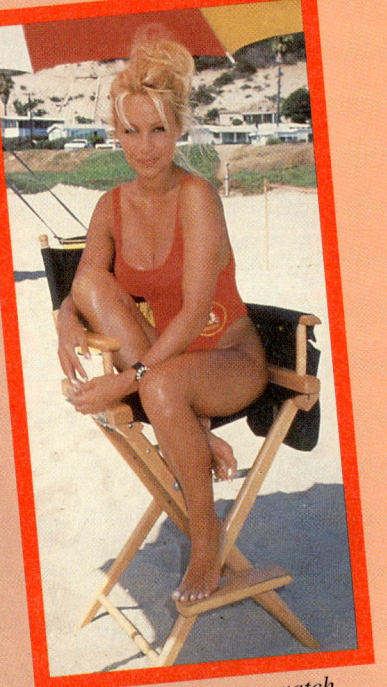

'*Baywatch* ... *Baaaaaywatch* ... *Baaaaaaywaaaatch* ...'

Months later, when the book deal was signed, we had calmed down enough to talk about what had happened. In private, hushed moments, we both admitted that we missed *Baywatch*.

'Sometimes I watch it late, when my girlfriend thinks I'm asleep,' Spitzy said.

'Yeah,' I said. 'I tell my roommate that it's just a joke. He's only caught me once.'

Neither of us ever spoke of David Sparks. We both knew he was never getting his precious tapes back — not while we lived and had breath. We had paid for those videocassettes. If not with blood, then with the tenuous fabric of our sanity. They were ours now, and no one could ever take them away from us.

# acknowledgments

As much as we'd like to take all the credit for putting this book together, there are a few people who must be recognized for their contributions. First and foremost, we thank John Rezek, our sugar daddy at *Playboy* magazine, who originally assigned us the task of making fun of *Baywatch*. Although he has refused to let us sleep over at his home and have pillow fights, he has been a constant source of inspiration and support. We also owe a huge debt of gratitude to our comely publisher, Michael O'Mara (or, as we know him, 'Shaft'), whose intelligence, generosity and obliging disposition have led us into manhood. He gave us Sally Potter, and we've tried not to break her. Love must also go out to David Sparks, the sucker who loaned us all of his *Baywatch* tapes and will probably never get them back; and Jane, Danielle and Patrick, our Holy Trinity of agents, who had faith in this book when we had fallen into heresy. A secret love goes out to Sandy Carter, the guy on the CIA information line, and several naughty *Baywatch* staffers: all of you did things you weren't supposed to do for us, and we hope you don't lose your jobs. Extra-special thanks go to Bruce Tracy, who didn't sue us for breach of contract, which we think is really swell.

    Spitznagel gives a hearty thanks to Kelly Kreglow, his partner in all things, who bravely sat through countless hours of *Baywatch* with him and helped him find 'The Funny.' He also thanks his family, for their love and patience, and the fine folks at Second City, who let him write on the job and showed such sincere interest in his work that he often felt more important than he actually was. Thanks are also due to Michael Grollman, his 'rich' friend who was always there to remind him that he was poor.

    Baber gives obedience and filial piety to the Great Father who rules over all and is ruled by none. He sends a grudging thanks to the illustrators and photo agents, who could have made his task more horrific and for the most part did not. And he's especially grateful to the Monks of the New Skete, who refrained from breaking his legs or beating him senseless over the money he still owes them.

    To anybody else we didn't mention (and we're sure there are a few), thanks for whatever it is you did for us. Bless your little pea-pickin' hearts. You're the gingiest.

The publishers are grateful to the following for permission to include the pictures reproduced on the pages indicated:

Abbas/Magnum Photos: p.122 (bottom left). APF/Corbis-Bettmann: p.50 (top). David Anderson/LGI Photo Agency: pp.11 (bottom), 77 (top). Miles Beck/LGI Photo Agency: p.77 (middle). Keith Butler/Rex Features Limited: p.46. Capital Pictures/LGI Photo Agency: pp.7 (top), 59 (top), 76 (left), 86 (right), 115 (bottom). Comstock, Inc.: pp.82 (left), 119. Corbis-Bettmann: pp.12, 19 (bottom), 24 (bottom), 28, 35 (top), 39 (top), 40 (bottom right), 41 (right), 83 (bottom), 84, 96 (main picture), 102, 105 (bottom). Corbis-Bettmann/Penguin: p.58 (right). Corbis-Bettmann/Springer: p.81 (bottom). Corbis/Everett: pp.44, 49 (bottom), 86 (middle). Corbis-Reuters/Bettmann: p.62. Elliott Erwitt/Magnum Photos: p.123 (middle). David Fisher/London Features: p.113 (bottom). M. Gerber: p.77 (bottom). Ronald Grant: pp.6, 16, 31 (main picture), 45 (top and bottom), 57 (bottom), 59 (bottom), 116 (bottom), 118. Tom Graves: pp.7, 21 (left), 24 (top), 32 (left), 33 (left and right), 34 (main picture), 37 (top and bottom), 40 (top and bottom left), 47 (bottom), 48 (top), 50 (bottom), 51 (top), 53 (top), 54, 58 (bottom), 72 (top), 79 (left), 81 (top), 85 (top), 88 (left), 89 (top), 94 (bottom), 101. Robert Harding Picture Library: pp.90 (top), 116 (top left). Sally Hobbs/Impact: p.112. Dave Hogan/Rex Features Limited: p.95 (right). Images Colour Library: pp.94, 96 (inset picture), 117. Chuck Jackson/LGI Photo Agency: p.10, 15 (top). Bill Kieffer: pp.74-5, 78, 98-9. The Kobal Collection/20th Century Fox: p.114 (middle). The Kobal Collection/Paramount: p.125. London Features: pp.35 (bottom), 63 (top), 69, 80, 82 (top), 95 (far left), 103 (bottom), 113 (top), 116 (top right), 127. Colin Mason/London Features: p.20 (bottom). Martin Parr/Magnum Photos: p.123 (top left). Pacha/LGI Photo Agency: p.93 (right). Photofest: pp.2, 22, 23 (right), 25, 27 (top), 29 (bottom), 30, 31 (insert picture), 38 (top), 39 (bottom), 47 (top left and right), 48 (bottom), 49 (top and middle), 51 (bottom), 52, 55 (right), 58 (insert picture), 63 (bottom and middle), 65, 66 (bottom right), 67 (top and middle), 68, 71 (bottom), 73 (top), 79 (left), 86 (left), 89 (bottom), 91 (left), 93 (left), 95 (left), 104, 106 (right), 113 (middle), 114 (bottom), 116 (left bottom), 117 (bottom), 122 (top left, middle and bottom right), 123 (top right and bottom right), 126. Popperfoto: pp.17, 32 (left), 56, 57 (top), 64, 73 (bottom). Rex Features Limited: p.70 (bottom). Tim Rooke/Rex Features Limited: pp.1, 34 (inset picture). Krista Roslof: pp.14 (top), 18, 23 (left), 26 (main picture), 42-3. Mark Skillicorn: pp.5, 14 (bottom), 36 (top and bottom), 60, 70 (top), 80 (top), 95, 100. Dennis Stone/Rex Features Limited: p.66 (left). Charles Sykes/Rex Features Limited: p.13 (bottom left). UPI/Corbis-Bettmann: pp.15 (bottom), 21 (right), 29 (top), 38 (bottom), 41 (middle), 53 (bottom), 55 (left), 61, 67 (bottom left), 72 (bottom), 76 (right), 83 (top), 85 (bottom), 88 (top), 90 (bottom), 91 (bottom), 92 (top), 103 (top), 105 (top), 106 (left), 114 (top), 121. Virgin Cola Company: p.13 (bottom right). Ron Wolfson/London Features: p.20 (top). Murray Wren: p.122 (top right). Zachary Present: pp.105-11.